Guide to

DEVELOPMENT of
PROTECTIVE SERVICES

for

OLDER PEOPLE

Guide to
DEVELOPMENT of
PROTECTIVE SERVICES
for
OLDER PEOPLE.

Edited by

GERTRUDE H. HALL

and

GENEVA MATHIASEN

With a Foreword by
Jack Ossofsky
Executive Director, The National Council on the Aging, Inc.

Published for

The National Council on the Aging

by

CHARLES C THOMAS · PUBLISHER
Springfield · Illinois · U.S.A.

Published and Distributed Throughout the World by
CHARLES C THOMAS • PUBLISHER
Bannerstone House
301-327 East Lawrence Avenue, Springfield, Illinois, U.S.A.

© 1973 by THE NATIONAL COUNCIL ON THE AGING, INC.
ISBN 0-398-02604-1—cloth
ISBN 398-02758-7—paper
Library of Congress Catalog Card Number: 72-88444

With THOMAS BOOKS *careful attention is given to all details of
manufacturing and design. It is the Publisher's desire to present books
that are satisfactory as to their physical qualities and artistic possibilities
and appropriate for their particular use.* THOMAS BOOKS *will be true
to those laws of quality that assure a good name and good will.*

Printed in the United States of America
W-2

Report of three community demonstration programs under the overall sponsorship of the National Council on the Aging, Inc., financed under Mental Health Project Grant MH 01540-04, National Institute of Mental Health, United States Department of Health, Education and Welfare.

GERTRUDE H. HALL, Project Director

GENEVA MATHIASEN, Former Executive Director, NCOA

THE NATIONAL COUNCIL ON THE AGING, INC.
1828 L Street, N.W., Washington, D.C. 20036

The National Council on the Aging, Inc. is a nonprofit corporation which serves as a central national resource for planning, informational materials, training, technical assistance and consultation in the field of older persons.

Foreword

T HIS VOLUME REPORTS the latest in a series of studies in Protective Services for Older People sponsored by the National Council on the Aging. The community demonstration programs reported here grew out of the recommendations of a National Seminar on Protective Services held in 1963 under the sponsorship of the National Council on the Aging with seven other voluntary organizations and federal agencies.

One hundred national leaders from medicine, social work, law, nursing and banking, who were concerned with these problems of the aging, defined protective services as:

> A constellation of services, preventive or supportive in nature, given with the purpose of helping these individuals to retain or achieve a level of competence and function to manage their own personal affairs or assets or both to the extent feasible, or with the purpose of acting on behalf of those incapable of managing for themselves.
>
> The identifying element of truly protective services is that there is present a readiness on the part of those rendering such services to use professional authority (which includes interventions), readiness to call legal authority into play, or readiness to operate under legal authority or legally sanctioned procedures . . . (as an accepting authority to act in behalf of an individual—to take responsibility for him).

At the National Seminar it became evident to the broad cross section of persons in attendance that guidelines for the development of protective services could be established only through tested experience. Subsequently, a demonstration project to be carried out in several communities was proposed. With a grant from the National Institute of Mental Health, the National Council on the Aging undertook the development of these demonstration projects in 1964.

Entailed in achieving the goal of this demonstration project were the following major tasks:

- Organization of a National Advisory Committee of Protective Services to establish policies, procedures and advise on recommendations, (subcommittees on selection of communities, legal aspects and evaluation).
- Establishment of requirements for local demonstrations.
- Selection of demonstration communities.
- Consultation and assistance to local sponsoring groups in developing plans and preparing protective service proposals for application grants.
- Formulation of a feasible evaluation plan.
- Providing current information and consultation on protective services to the local prospective demonstration projects, as well as other local, state and national agencies which requested assistance.

Conclusions reached in each of the project demonstration explorations called for a coordinated community plan as the most feasible approach to providing the multiplicity of services essential to the protection of impaired older people. To provide an effective network of the legal, medical and psychosocial services required, new patterns of coordination and collaboration had to be initiated. The major problem which became evident in the development of each of the protective service demonstrations was how to bring together several agencies in a cooperative scheme in such a manner as to maximize their contributions without threatening or impairing the autonomy of each.

It was agreed by the project planners that to locate, reach and serve the "hard-to-reach" impaired older persons required not only a wide range of resources and flexibility, but also the experimentation with new approaches in dealing with older people.

The demonstration programs described here indicate that no single model can be prescribed for replication in all communities. They do provide a variety of approaches and experiences which we believe will serve as useful guides to the many communities now concerned with providing services for older persons in need of protection.

It is the belief of the National Council on the Aging that

an effective program of protective service will not only help individual elderly persons but may also point the way toward development of an integrated approach to services and care of the aging and initiate improved methods for locating and helping the impaired older person. Such a program suggests a departure from the single agency approach of a problem to a cooperative-collaborative community approach, wherein several agencies and disciplines pool their resources, new patterns for the delivery of service to older people who have need for protection and more acceptable methods of offering services to the growing numbers of all older people.

The demonstration programs represent creative contributions of countless people across the country. It is impossible to mention them all by name. The thanks of the National Council on the Aging go first of all to Gertrude H. Hall, the Project Director, who gave four years of devoted service to helping develop the demonstration programs and to increasing national concern about the growing need for protective service. Special commendation must be given also to the directors of the local projects: Mrs. Pauline DeWolf, San Diego; Mrs. Agnes McRoberts, Houston; and Mr. John Steward, Philadelphia. The energy, skill, humanity and persistence of the Project Directors and staff members produced whatever of value resulted from the program.

The National Advisory Committee under the chairmanship of Professor Hugh Allan Ross, Thomas Franklin Backus School of Law, Case Western Reserve University, gave valuable guidance throughout the project. A final word of thanks goes to Geneva Mathiasen, retired Executive Director of the National Council on the Aging, who edited the final report, and to Ollie A. Randall, who served as special assistant to the Project Director.

JACK OSSOFSKY
Executive Director, NCOA

CONTENTS

TABLES

Guide to

DEVELOPMENT of
PROTECTIVE SERVICES

for

OLDER PEOPLE

Chapter I

Protecting Elderly Persons in the Community

WHAT A PROTECTIVE SERVICE PROGRAM IN A COMMUNITY CAN DO

INCREASED LIFE EXPECTANCY in the twentieth century has given many Americans added years of life. For some it has become a time for leisure, creativity and fulfillment. These are the fortunate older persons who have at least moderately good health, enough income for basic needs, interested friends and/or relatives, and opportunities for sociability, usefulness and continuing interests.

There are also impaired elderly individuals who are alone, without close relatives or friends, and fearful of losing control over their own lives. These are the persons, often widowed, usually over seventy-five years of age, who present the greatest number of medical, psychiatric and social problems. They constitute the group to whom the three protective service demonstration programs reported in this volume addressed themselves. They are the least attractive, the most debilitated of the elderly group and are often neglected even by members of helping professions who do not know what to do for or with them, because few have had enough experience with rehabilitation of older people to understand their potential for improvement.

It is fortunate, therefore, that these three demonstration projects were so frequently able to verify the resilience of the lifelong strengths of older people when they are assisted by professional and nonprofessional workers who have the skill and commitment to help older people according to their individual needs. In many instances, an individual who appeared to be a

3

hopeless aged person in an untenable situation responded to protective services and was restored to enjoy the remaining years of his life.

It was not possible to save all who were referred to the projects. There were some older people, victims of severe neglect, who were found too late, when illness, accident or other misfortune had rendered their condition irreversible.

A summary appraisal of what a protective service program can realistically hope to do suggests the following:

- It is possible to locate and serve hard-to-reach older persons who need protection. The number who can be found and helped depends on commitment, availability of funds, community resources, appropriate personnel and a sound plan for a protective service delivery system.
- Most of the impaired and often despairing older people can be made more comfortable, and many will gradually achieve self-esteem and a measure of self-direction.
- The majority of marginally competent older persons can be protected without a declaration of incompetency or loss of liberty.
- Some hostile older persons who may appear to be dangerously incompetent can be helped to return to more satisfying ways of life. A change in the environmental situation, compatible with the individual's needs and capacity, may lead to reestablishment of positive personal relationships and sometimes to reuniting of families.
- Members of the helping professions (attorneys, judges, nurses, physicians, social workers) who engage in a collaborative effort of providing protective services gain an understanding of the impaired older person which modifies traditional practice and promotes flexibility in resolving the problems of protection.
- Protective service programs can be carried out by a variety of agencies. The essential ingredients are (a) a commitment to provide or secure and coordinate those services and facilities needed for the protection and well-being of the increasing number of elderly persons and (b) skilled and

resourceful personnel able to work in collaboration with other professions and with impaired older persons.

- A protective service program is expected (a) to assess the needs of elderly persons for service and living arrangements; (b) to identify the kinds of care needed; and (c) to obtain the services which will enable persons to continue to live independently as long as possible or which will provide protective living arrangements and care appropriate to the needs of those for whom independent living is no longer possible.

PROGRESS TOWARD MEETING THE NEED FOR PROTECTION

In 1958, a small ad hoc committee called together by the National Council on the Aging (NCOA) agreed that the need of many elderly persons for some kind of protective service was urgent and that it was receiving little attention.

Ten years later, at the end of the research and demonstration projects reported here, less than twenty communities in the entire country could be identified as having community-wide protective service programs for the aged. This would appear to be slow progress indeed. In the intervening years, the number of persons over seventy-five most likely to need protection has increased significantly. More and more manifestations of disturbed or disordered behavior and of exploitation, untended illness and neglect have come to the attention of police, social workers, physicians, nurses, lawyers, postmen, insurance agents, trust officers, social security and public welfare offices, unions, fire departments, neighbors and the general public. Such slow progress is undoubtedly due, in large part, to the complicated nature of the problem and to traditional attitudes which accept deviant behavior as normal for an older person. It has been clear from the initial discussions of the subject that to provide protective service is uncommonly difficult, demanding and frustrating.

Little documented experience is available to provide communities with guidelines for organizing and providing protective service programs for older adults. There has, however, been a succession of events in the last decade which has helped to define the nature of protective service more precisely, to identify the resources which are basic to carrying it out and to refine the methods and personnel most likely to succeed.

Programs of Research and Demonstration

Following the 1958 ad hoc committee meeting, NCOA began a study of the social and legal implications of protective service under the direction of Virginia Lehman, who was a trained practitioner both as an attorney and as a social worker. She had had personal experience with a protective service program in Chicago as a member of the staff of the Legal Aid Society. The report of her study was published in 1963 under the title, *Guardianship and Protective Services for Older People.*

Using this book as a text, a seminar on protective services was arranged with the announced purpose of drawing up guidelines for providing a community-based protective service program. The seminar was jointly sponsored by seven national agencies, federal and voluntary, with concern and/or responsibility for elderly persons. Participants included representatives of the social work, medical and legal professions. The prepared papers and discussions provided new ideas and additional information, but the seminar did not produce guidelines. It became clear that there was insufficient experience in working with elderly impaired persons to justify an attempt to draw up specific recommendations for action, though the published proceedings made a useful addition to the small body of literature on the subject.

It was proposed that NCOA sponsor a group of coordinated community programs which would maintain comparable records of experience and might provide a realistic basis for guidelines to other community groups. The outcome of that proposal is reported in this volume.

In the meantime, several other important events have occurred. In 1964, Benjamin Rose Institute, an agency providing a wide range of services exclusively for older people in Cleveland, Ohio, undertook a research project in protective service, financed by the Social Security Administration. A number of progress reports and papers based on the project have added new insights into the nature of the protective service client and the service itself.

In 1967, the Social and Rehabilitation Service of the Department of Health, Education and Welfare initiated a project to demonstrate protective service programs in public welfare. The project was based on two demonstration programs: one in three rural counties in Colorado; the other in the city of Washington, D.C. A report of the project was published in 1971 to encourage and assist state and local welfare departments to carry out the federal mandate to provide protective services.*

A number of state and local conferences and meetings have been held. The Veterans Administration has held institutes in various parts of the country, investigating better methods of dealing with elderly veterans, many of whom have need for protection. A number of national organizations have included protective service as part of their ongoing conference programs, among them the American Public Welfare Association, the National Conference on Social Welfare and the Family Service Association of America.

Three meetings organized by NCOA as adjuncts to its protective service demonstration program are reported fully in NCOA publications.† Two are summarized here as having significance for any community development of protective service for aged persons.

The Law and the Impaired Older Person—The Lake Case

This report is based on the legal brief and the decision of the Court of Appeals, in the case of *Catherine Lake v. Dale Cameron,* Superintendent of St. Elizabeth's Hospital, a federal hospital for the mentally ill in the District of Columbia. Catherine

---

* U.S. *Social and Rehabilitation Service: Report of the National Protective Service Project for Older Adults.* Washington, D.C., U.S. Dept. Health, Education and Welfare, 1971.

† *The Law and the Impaired Older Person: Protection or Punishment. Overcoming Barriers to Protective Services for the Aged. A Crucial Issue in Social Work Practice: Protective Services for Older People.*

Lake had become an involuntary patient in the hospital for some four years, after a police officer found her wandering in the streets unable to give her address. She was taken to the police station and shortly afterward to St. Elizabeth's Hospital where she was found by the Mental Health Commission to be dangerous to herself and thus qualified for commitment. The court, therefore, signed an order finding her to be insane and committed her to the hospital. She protested the finding and, aided by a sister, tried various legal means to secure her release, without success. Finally, Chief Judge Bazelon of the Court of Appeals granted a rehearing of Mrs. Lake's application for a writ of habeas corpus which had been dismissed by the trial court. Mr. Hyman Smollar, a Washington attorney, after consulting with NCOA about the issues involved, agreed to serve as attorney for the appellant. The case for her defense centered around the following points:

1. The Mentally Ill Act of the District of Columbia provides for hospitalization or "any other alternative course of treatment which the court believes will be in the best interests of the person or the public."
2. If there had been money in the family to provide for her care and supervision, she would not have been committed; hence, hospital confinement with loss of civil rights was a result of impoverishment.
3. She had admittedly not received any psychiatric treatment in the hospital.

Judge George Bowles of the Circuit Court, Wayne County, Michigan, commenting on the brief, said the following: "If there would eventuate from this case the principle that trial judge . . . would have an affirmative obligation to seek out and exhaust alternative means (to commitment), this would indeed be a landmark. . . ." The decision of the court handed down on May 19, 1966, was in favor of the defendant, and the case was remanded to the district court "for an inquiry into *other alternative courses of treatment.*"

The Lake case applies legally only to the District of Columbia, though the moral application can be interpreted nationwide. The significant factor in the decision may, in the long run, be the placing of legal responsibility for alternative resources for care of mentally impaired elderly persons squarely on the community.

Overcoming Barriers to Protective Services for the Aged

In 1967, informal conversations among professional persons directly involved with programs or problems of protective service indicated a need for a series of planned discussions by practitioners. It was evident that many communities were experiencing difficulty in arousing public interest and financial support for protective service programs. A small group which convened in Washington, D.C. recommended that a meeting be organized around the theme of "Overcoming Barriers to Protective Service for the Elderly." Subsequently, an institute bearing this title was held in Houston, Texas, in January 1968. It was jointly sponsored by seven federal and voluntary agencies. The participants were limited to fifty, of whom at least half were actively working in protective service programs. All the professions essential to the service were well represented. Discussions were based on case histories of protective service clients submitted by the sponsoring organizations. The main thrust was to stimulate more rapid growth of protective service programs in communities across the country by identifying barriers to securing the collaborative effort and the range of services necessary to resolve the problems of protection.

At the opening session, it was clear that there was considerable confusion even among practitioners as to what protective services entail, and no definition so far proposed was acceptable to the entire group. As an outgrowth of the workshop discussions, a small committee prepared a statement (which has received wide acceptance) of the elements of a protective service program. This committee pointed out that confusion arose because of the fact that most services in the social, health and legal professions are in a sense "protective." The lawyer and social worker "protects" his client, as the doctor does his patient. The true protective service program, it was pointed out, combines three types of service: preventive, supportive and surrogate. The potential for surrogate service is the distinguishing feature of a protective service for elderly persons not able to act on their own behalf, but it does not come into play in every case. Nor does surrogate service necessarily mean judicial proceedings, guardianship or conservatorship. It may mean acting on behalf of an individual unable to exercise sound judgment, to remove him from an environment considered dangerous, to arrange for a medical or psychiatric examination or for admission to a hospital or nursing home. If appropriate preventive and supportive services are available to the protective service workers and if the endangering situation can be discovered in time, the potential need to exercise the surrogate function may not eventuate or it may be temporary. The surrogate function of a protective service agency may not necessarily continue throughout the life of a client. With appropriate medical and social services, the person may regain ability to make his own decisions; he may come to trust the protective service worker's judgment and concur in actions which he previously resisted. If the need for surrogate service continues over a substantial period of time, a relative or friend may be located who can appropriately assume the surrogate responsibility.

The Houston Institute on Protective Service concluded that "Essential to the development of protection for older people is the establishment of a Protective Service System which will provide comprehensive services according to the changing needs of older people as they may require assistance in daily living, health care or management of their affairs. This System will include a broad range of preventive, supportive and surrogate services which may be provided by a variety of individual agencies and institutions."

Programs Related to Protective Service

In addition to the programs already mentioned, many examples of service and research not identified specifically as protective service have contributed greatly to better understanding of the impaired older person and alternate methods of giving him help. Reports of such studies as those of the Langley Porter

Institute,* the Group for the Advancement of Psychiatry† and the legal profession‡ provide evidence of significant new professional tools for protective service agencies and their professional personnel.

If to these studies are added the reports of research and demonstration in the field of practice, it is clear that a great deal of information is now available on service needs of older people and methods of providing preventive and supportive services.§

NCOA Demonstration Project

Immediately following the seminar on Protective Service which recommended a group of coordinated community programs, NCOA began to explore the possibilities of such a project. The process, problems and results of that undertaking are described in ensuing chapters.

Much has been learned from the NCOA demonstration programs to give encouragement and practical help to community leaders who recognize the necessity of developing resources to protect elderly impaired persons no longer able, alone, to make wise decisions about the management of their property and/or their lives. New insights will come as shared experience continues. It is clear from the candid reporting of both success and failure and from descriptions of varying attitudes and approaches to the problems encountered in these three programs that only a few guidelines can be formulated and no one model program be presented.

AIMS AND PRINCIPLES OF A PROTECTIVE SERVICE PROGRAM

Usually, the individual becomes known to the protective service agency at the time of danger or imminent crisis, a victim

---

* Lowenthal, M.; Beckman, P. *et al.*: *Aging and Mental Disorder in San Francisco.* San Francisco, Jossey Bass, 1967.

† Group for the Advancement of Psychiatry: *Laws Governing Hospitalization of the Mentally Ill.* Formulated by the Committee on Psychiatry and the Law. New York, 1966, Vol. 6, Report No. 61.

‡ Allen, Richard C.: *Mental Impairment and Legal Incompetency.* New York, Prentice-Hall, 1968.

§ See also Bibliography, Appendix I.

of what Dr. Herbert Weiss has called "the harm of neglect." The protective service worker attempts to assess the condition of the person and his environment, calling for such other professional assistance as the situation dictates. The ultimate aim is to mobilize the individual's own remaining strengths and to utilize whatever resources are available in the community to improve his ability to function and to live out whatever remains of his life in safety and dignity, with as much satisfaction, enjoyment and comfort as possible. Sometimes removal from a hazardous environment or securing prompt medical care prolongs life. The basic concern of the protective service is, however, that of improving the quality of life, rather than survival in an untenable situation.

Basic Principles of Protection

There are four overriding principles which influence the decision about the appropriate action to be taken in giving protective service to elderly persons.

- So far as possible, the client participates in making the decision as to the action which should be taken to meet his needs.
- The client is helped to "remain in the community" so long as his condition warrants it and to "return to the community" as soon as possible after hospitalization or care in some type of protective facility.
- Surrogate action is taken by a professionally responsible person if the person is incapable of making a decision and there is no responsible relative or friend to make it for him or if he refuses to concur in action deemed necessary to protect him or other persons from harm. (If force is necessary, a court order is required in most states.)
- When surrogate action is taken, involving loss of civil rights or rights of self-direction, they are restored or instituted as soon as the situation warrants. It is not to be assumed that an individual's lack of competence to direct his own affairs is permanent. Such conditions as physical illness, malnutrition or shock of bereavement may cause

temporary inability to exercise good judgment or take any action no matter how necessary. If the need is discovered in time, treatment and support often restore the individual's ability to manage his own affairs.

Realistic Anticipations of Successful Outcome

In view of the extremely critical situation of most protective service clients and their frequently expressed desire to be left alone, the question is sometimes raised about the validity of protective service as a priority community program. The protective service workers in the three demonstration programs were impressed by the number of cases presumed to be hopeless in which radical improvements were achieved. Many sick, confused and minimally functioning elderly men and women responded positively to the services designed by the program to meet their individual needs, and they quite literally gained a new life.

However, not all protective service cases result in restoration or improvement in ability to function. Some came to the attention of the agency too late. Sometimes the essential community resources and services were not available. Sometimes the professional judgment of persons inexperienced in providing protective service may have been imperfect. Intervention may have been postponed too long. Many times, the entrance of the protective service worker into the situation marked a turning point. Unknown facts came to light. Relatives and friends were discovered. With care and treatment, health improved. Humane interest and practical help changed attitudes which appeared unchangeable. In some cases, involuntary intervention enabled the elderly person to secure the things he really wanted most at the end of his life. This seems to have been so in the cases summarized below.* These five were selected as representing individuals whose problems were unusually severe at the time they were referred to protective service and whose situations improved markedly as a result of the help they received.

------

* Narrative descriptions of the results emanating from the protective services provided these and other individuals in the demonstration program are described in more detail in Appendix II, Case Histories.

Five Examples of Change

An angry, hostile man of seventy-eight, considered danger-ously incompetent, long estranged from his family and a partial amputee with a history of tuberculosis, was found critically ill in a rat-infested slum. He became a pleasant, distinguished-looking grandfather with a concerned family, new interests and a profitable craft and lived near his daughter in a nursing home where he received appropriate medical care.

A woman, eighty-two, found unconscious and near starvation, had been separated from her family since childhood. She was illiterate, frightened and alone, and too weak to get her last $150 from the bank. Later she changed to a dignified, self-respecting lady in a starched white apron, whose residence in a home for the aged was financed by a prosperous younger brother, proud to care for and to visit his only living sister, long presumed dead.

A man of sixty-eight, living in a nursing home with almost total loss of memory following a stroke, no known family, friends or source of income, went back to his old neighborhood and friends. He became a man with a small bank account, new clothes and his funeral paid for and lived in a home of an old and trusted friend whose school teacher daughter served as his guardian.

A woman, sixty-eight, exhibiting disturbed, bizarre and finan-cially extravagant behavior following the death of her husband, was taken in restraint for psychiatric examination. She soon became a woman capable of some self-care, when her condition, caused by an inoperable brain abnormality, was stabilized under medical care and supervision and when she went to live in the home of a brother (who became her guardian) and sister-in-law who had moved to the city in which she lived to give her more personal attention.

A man, eighty-one, formerly a successful photographer, a hostile chronic alcoholic following the death of his wife, was evicted by his landlord after he had set fire to the house and was removed to a hospital by force. He again became a man of recognized brilliance and creativity, contributing to magazines and starting to write a book, after he became a resident in a nursing home where he received appropriate continuing medical care for a rare, severe and previously undiagnosed kidney ailment.

The Meaning of "Living in the Community"

It will be noted that at the end of the cases summarized above, two of the persons were living in nursing homes following hospital treatment; one was in a home for the aged; one lived in a foster home with an old friend; one had gone to live with her brother and sister-in-law.

All needed help with the activities of daily living, and most needed medical and personal supervision. None had living spouses. None was living in his own home. The extent to which they can be considered as having been "returned to the community" depends on a clearer definition of a phrase which has become a euphemism for living outside an institution. Arranging admission to nursing homes or "foster homes" for persons being released from mental hospitals, for example, is often referred to as "returning them to the community." A nursing or even a foster home may provide little contact with the "community" outside the premises.

For protective service clients with mental and physical impairment, living in one's own home often means living alone, with community contacts depending on neighbors or other individuals to help with activities of daily living (cleaning, shopping and food preparation, personal care, et cetera). If facilities are available in the community to provide such services in the home, many persons prefer the privacy of their own homes in spite of possible social isolation. However, many communities do not have the variety of supportive services such as home health aides, homemaker, housekeeper, visiting aides, home-delivered meals, visiting nurse, et cetera, which are often required for an elderly impaired person to live a quasi-independent, safe and healthful life "in the community." Thus, it may be that for many elderly people the sense of "living in the community" depends not so much on the place of residence as on maintaining meaningful relationships with individuals who comprise their community.

SUMMARY

While it is evident that protective service programs have been slow in development, much has been learned about the need for the service and the elements which contribute to successful achievement in working with impaired elderly persons. Experience in protective service programs indicated that great care must be taken in moving even gravely disabled older persons from their home to care and treatment in institutions. Experience also demonstrated that some of the most severely impaired and deteriorated persons have been rehabilitated in institutions and restored to non-institutional living and self-care.

A better understanding of the various types of services and facilities needed in the community to provide appropriate care both in the home and in institutions is essential if the protection needed by increasing numbers of people who reach advanced age is to be provided.

Chapter II

Organizing the Protective Service Project

T HE NATIONAL COUNCIL on the Aging undertook the organization and supervision of a series of programs of protective service on the theory expressed in the project proposal that "from a variety of demonstration projects, functioning separately and independently, but recognized as parts of a total program, experience would be gained which could give guidance to the entire country." The project was financed by the National Institute of Mental Health for a period of three years (later extended to four years).

"At present," the proposal stated, "there is a recognized need, but there is practically no movement toward actually dealing with a situation which grows daily more acute. The type of program here proposed would provide impetus and guidance for effective action."

THE PLAN

The organization plan provided that NCOA would do the following:

- Identify a number of communities with an active interest in establishing a program of protective services for older people.
- After field visits and consultations, choose five of these communities for the demonstration.
- Help each community to prepare a plan for providing protective services and to design a request for financial support from a national or local foundation, an appropriate governmental agency or a combination of these sources.
- Following the progress of each program through field visits

17

and reports and give assistance as needed and requested.

- Arrange for periodic meetings of representatives of the programs to compare experiences and exchange ideas.
- Prepare methods of record-keeping and objective evaluation of results, in order to distill from the total experience those factors which would be most likely to assist other communities.
- Disseminate information about results through periodic and final reports.

Although the project did not work out altogether as planned, a candid report of the attempts to get community programs established is given in some deail in the belief that a record of problems and setbacks as well as of achievements and successes may be helpful.

Guidelines for the Local Demonstrations

The broad plans for the NCOA Protective Service Project were reviewed by a National Advisory Committee under the chairmanship of Hugh Allan Ross, Professor of Law, Case Western Reserve University, Cleveland.* The committee worked out criteria for the selection of project communities, application forms and the method of evaluation of project proposals.

Sixteen community agencies presented full applications. Correspondence with these agencies and visits to fourteen of the communities led to reduction of the number to ten potential demonstration programs to be considered by the subcommittee on selections. This preliminary survey provided some clues to community planning:

- Community planning councils, social security offices and public welfare or public health departments appeared to be the agencies most frequently mobilizing interest in protective services for older people.
- Social service departments of veterans' hospitals, family service agencies and coordinating committees on the aging, also participated actively in preliminary planning.

---

* See Appendix III for a complete list of the members of the Advisory Committee.

- The original material distributed by NCOA to prospective applicants suggested a wide variety of sponsoring agencies. On-site visits and consultations indicated that there were few existing single agencies with the combination of commitment, expertise and flexibility to carry out a program which would deal with some of the most difficult social and health problems in the community. Collaborative efforts of a number of different agencies and professions would be required.

Criteria for Selection

Six communities which appeared to have the greatest potential for the development of a demonstration were chosen by the committee, based on the following criteria:

- Readiness to participate in such a demonstration.
- Resources and leadership which gave promise to the community's ability to organize quickly to carry out the demonstration.
- Flexibility and capacity to cooperate in a program involving other communities and requiring a system of recording and reporting.
- Commitment to a protective service program and to continuation of the local program at the end of the demonstration.

The following were the six communities and agencies:

- *Boston*—United Community Services of Metropolitan Boston, with the cooperation of the Tenant and Community Relations Department of the Housing Authority and three voluntary casework agencies.
- *Chicago*—Welfare Council of Metropolitan Chicago, with cooperation of local and state mental health departments. Active leadership, support and staff assistance with casework services were offered by three public and four voluntary agencies.
- *Houston*—Sheltering Arms, a voluntary agency serving older people exclusively, with the sanction of many other health and social agencies in the community.

- *Jefferson County, Colorado*—Metropolitan Council for Community Services, Denver, and the county public welfare department, with the cooperation of two other public and one voluntary agency concerned with the problems of older people.
- *Philadelphia*—City Department of Public Welfare, with cooperation of other community agencies concerned with protection of older people.
- *San Diego*—Community Welfare Council of San Diego and the School of Social Work, San Diego State College, with active interest of the county public welfare department and four voluntary casework agencies.

In spite of the best efforts of many lay and professional leaders, representing voluntary and government agencies at local, state and federal levels, projects were actually carried out in only three of these communities. Therefore, a brief review of the process involved in program planning and funding is presented here, together with some analysis of the problems involved.

COMMUNITY PROBLEMS

Funding

Initially, the local sponsoring groups did not consider funding would be a particularly difficult problem. Three of the communities believed they could secure funds locally. However, a shortage or previous commitment of United Community funds and other voluntary resources for financing was found to be a major stumbling block in developing a new community service with voluntary funding, even in those places where surveys had shown a critical and growing need for protective measures for older people. Government funding appeared more favorable. At the outset, it was believed that a single federal source would provide funding for all the demonstrations. However, by the time the NCOA project had been approved and funded, this plan was not feasible.

A second plan was formulated, calling for cooperative funding under a "package agreement" with several federal agencies jointly funding the local demonstrations. The idea was received with interest at a meeting of representatives of potential federal granting agencies. However, it became clear that such joint action was not practicable because of varying policies and procedures in the government agencies. It was suggested that with the assistance of NCOA, each local agency should make application for funding to a federal agency, with no overlapping or competition for funds.

NCOA agreed to give assistance in preparation of the grant proposals. Guidelines for materials to be included in the grant request and an outline of requirements to insure an appropriate degree of uniformity were sent to each of the potential sponsoring agencies.

One community, Houston, was able to secure grants from two local foundations which enabled the program to become operative within a short time.

A second community, after working with foundations over a period of months without success, decided to approach several federal agencies at the same time. Here, the group was confronted with the need to conform to different specifications and application forms for each of the granting agencies. Formulating the funding requests became a major undertaking. NCOA offered the assistance of a professional project writer. After innumerable consultations and draft proposals, the local planners decided to change the sponsoring agency and the site of the demonstration. Eventually, a planning grant was obtained from the U.S. Public Health Service. It gradually became clear, however, that a program which involved coordination among several agencies, including a hospital and a public housing project, could not be achieved, and ultimately the planning grant was returned.

A third community confidently expected a local foundation grant and continued hopeful for some time. However, for various reasons, including staff changes, these funds proved unavailable. It was then proposed that the county welfare department join the community council in sponsorship, with funding to be requested from the Department of Health, Education and Welfare. Considerable effort was made to work out a feasible plan. Eventually, the State Department of Public Welfare decided to apply for participation in the Protective Service Demonstration Project of the Social and Rehabilitation Service in the Department of Health, Education and Welfare. This was a program for protective services to older adults to be conducted by local departments of public welfare with 100 percent federal financing. The application was accepted and the program, carried out in three counties in another part of the state, became one of the two participants in this federally sponsored program.*

The three other communities, among the six which had been selected, decided from the outset to approach one of the federal agencies which had earlier expressed an interest in the possibility of funding a local protective service demonstration. Details of these experiences need not be reported here. Consultations were held with national, regional, state and sometimes local representatives of the federal agencies. Applications were prepared and revised. Budgets were reduced, increased and reduced again. Occasionally, different recommendations were received from regional and national offices. Changes in appropriations and in the federal agencies' program emphasis created unavoidable delays. Inordinate amounts of effort were required in the negotiations, and local interest was difficult to maintain.

One community agency, after receiving what it considered assurance of approval, employed a well-qualified project director. Subsequent changes in the personnel of the federal agency review committee necessitated further changes in the grant proposal, with an added period of delay, during which the project director and another potential director accepted other positions. Finally the project was rejected, ostensibly on the grounds that at that time a well-qualified person was not available to direct the project. This program was eventually funded by the federal agency and is now in progress, but it was too late to include it in the NCOA project.

It should be recognized that the granting agencies had valid reasons for viewing with some skepticism grant proposals which

---

* The fact that this national project for Protective Services in Public Welfare was originally planned to include a minimum of three community projects provides further evidence of difficulties involved in initiating protective service programs.

called for creation of new agencies or new patterns of delivery of service, which could not be specific about many aspects of operation and which involved active collaboration of a variety of groups and disciplines, some of which lay outside the special program emphasis of the granting agency.

Some community leaders became discouraged by the difficult and time-consuming efforts of funding protective service programs and decided to focus their energies on less innovative, better established programs, which were easier to explain and for which funding was less difficult.

Two committees were successful in obtaining government grants. The San Diego project was funded with two grants: one from the Administration on Aging in the Department of Health, Education and Welfare and another from the California Commission on Aging, under Title III of the Older Americans Act. The federal portion of the grant was for the research aspect of the program and the state portion for the service aspect.

The City Department of Public Welfare in Philadelphia received a grant from the Pennsylvania Department of Public Welfare, financed in part by Title III funds of the Older Americans Act and in part by state funds.

Thus for NCOA project purposes, the six communities accepted for the demonstration programs were reduced to three: Houston, San Diego and Philadelphia.

Organization

Through the process of working out specific program proposals, community and agency leaders began to understand the seriousness and complexity of the problems confronting protective service clients and the demands which would be made on any agency accepting responsibility for this type of clientele.

Elderly impaired individuals in need of protection have not traditionally been served in substantial numbers by health and social agencies. Many practitioners in social work and other helping professions had been unaware of the existence of persons revealing such severe deprivation and neglect. Some well-intentioned and concerned persons, including professionals in medicine, social work and the law, tended at first to write off the elderly people in need of protective service as hopeless. They were seen as people suffering from "chronic brain syndrome" who should be confined to mental hospitals; as skid-row alcoholics for whom a flophouse is the only solution; or as people whose acted-out hostility and aggression justify immediate police and court procedures.

Others feared that little could be accomplished without a network of social and health services and resources, some of which were unavailable in the community; or they were discouraged by the fragmentation of such services as did exist and the lack of communication and cooperation among agencies which tend to focus on providing a single service rather than on the service needs of the whole person.

The problem of potential legal intervention was particularly difficult. Agency administrators and boards were concerned about becoming entangled in legal matters. Social workers have been imbued with the traditional social work concept of client self-determination. Joint action involving social work and the law has been rare, for elderly people especially.

Finally, there was reluctance to change patterns of service. Agencies and individuals use the words "cooperation" and "coordination" easily. However, developing team effort on an operating basis without threatening autonomy or sharing what is conceived of as a mandated or assigned area of responsibility and authority is another matter. Hospitals, for example, contend they must be the sole judges of admission and release of patients and must assume total control of the patient's care while he is in the hospital. However, a protective service social worker has a strong sense of responsibility not to return a patient to a loathsome environment, though the hospital authorities in need of the bed may require his immediate removal. Case records show numerous instances in which patients' needs were disregarded because the gears of the machinery designed to help people did not mesh. For example, protective service patients were sometimes dismissed and sent home alone without notification to the protective service agency.

The guidelines for the local programs stressed the necessity for cooperative relationships among social workers, doctors, lawyers, the police; a variety of institutions, including courts, hospitals, nursing homes, mental hospitals, mental health centers, visiting nurse associations, homemaker and home health aide agencies; and a variety of public agencies, especially departments of public health, public welfare and housing.

Some community and agency leaders, after initial exploration, became appalled and discouraged by the enormity and complexity of the problems involved in initiating and coordinating a protective service program, and their enthusiasm waned. Others viewed the program as a necessity and a challenge with implications for delivery of health and social services in other programs as well.

Securing Quality Staff

In all the projects, locating persons qualified to work effectively with protective service clients posed special difficulties. Recommended qualifications for project directors included a master's degree in social work and experience in community organization, agency administration and social casework. In addition, a commitment to helping impaired older people was necessary, as well as the ability to develop positive working relationships with the elderly clients and with the variety of professional and semiprofessional persons whose cooperation was essential.

Employment of qualified social workers and case aides also presented problems. It was particularly difficult to ascertain in advance whether a worker would be able to relate effectively to impaired older persons, who may be much more difficult for some persons to work with than are younger clients.

In view of the complicated nature of the work and the responsibilities involved, NCOA recommended that staff salaries be budgeted at 10 to 20 percent above the local rate for comparable positions. However, none of the projects was able to establish such a salary scale. This fact may account for the turnover of staff in two of the projects.

OPERATIONAL RESEARCH AND EVALUATION PROGRAM

A unified system of recording and reporting was established, and detailed case records were kept. Information was gathered in the following areas:

- *The Protective Service Client.* Analysis and classification of individuals were based on functional capacity and environmental conditions. (The classifications worked out in the projects helped to identify and describe discernible groups in what appeared to be a disparate mass of individuals in deep trouble. They provided a framework for determining to what extent a situation was due to individual incapacity or to environmental conditions. The classifications also served as bench marks to measure progress and change as a result of services provided through the program.) Objective evidences of change were recorded by noting characteristics at the time of initial contact, at the end of the first month, at the end of the third month and—for long-term clients— at the end of the seventh, eighth or ninth month.

- *Nature and Extent of Service.* The nature and volume of the service, including the extent of need for involuntary intervention, were recorded as well as the service needs, met and unmet.

- *Use of Professional Personnel.* The amount of time spent by social workers and case aides and the use of professional help from other disciplines were recorded.

- *Extent of Need.* In the original plan, it was hoped that the protective service program could be limited, at least in some communities, to a specific geographical area, with intensive outreach and case-finding and saturation of service, in order to arrive at some estimate of the number of persons in need of protective service and perhaps also to assess the number of those in precarious situations who might be helped to avoid a crisis through preventive and supportive services, given directly or through referral to other appropriate sources of help. This plan did not prove to be practical, since in each of the demonstrations the service was made available to the entire community. Some inferences were drawn as to the potential need for service based on the numbers served, but no firm data could be secured about the relationship of the numbers served to the total community need.*

Evaluation Problems

The period of reporting for the evaluation program was set for the calendar year 1967. A major complication of the research element in the project was the timing of the three demonstration programs. The Houston program was underway at the beginning of 1966. The Philadelphia program was funded in late 1966, but problems of staffing and turnover made it necessary to modify the reporting system. The San Diego project was not fully staffed until May 1967.

The Houston program tested the schedules in 1966 and participated in the research and evaluation plan from January 1 to December 31, 1967, after a year of experience. The San Diego records were available for a nine-month period. A portion of the Philadelphia findings were gleaned from an analysis of case material rather than from the research schedules. While this divergence was a handicap to securing comparative data from the three projects, certain differences in results reported appeared to depend to a large extent on the length of time a program had been in operation. These differences were significant enough to suggest that a year's time is necessary to get a protective service program to a fully functioning stage.

---

* Copies of record and report forms as well as other guidelines sent to the local communities are available on request to The National Council on the Aging.

Chapter III

The Demonstration Communities, Sponsoring Agencies and Protective Service Programs

COMMUNITY AND AGENCY CHARACTERISTICS

THE PLAN FOR A number of protective service programs in different parts of the country, in different kinds of communities and under different types of auspices, was based on the desire to learn the extent to which such external factors might influence the need for and provision of protective service.

As the total nature of a protective service is understood to include preventive and supportive as well as surrogate services, understanding grows about the importance of community resources. These include adequate housing; health and social services designed to help people remain in their own homes; a central information and referral resource; and a constellation of institutional facilities to provide for emergency, short-term, extended or permanent care—all based on a philosophy of restoration and rehabilitation. Most communities do not have all these resources, and the demonstration communities were no exceptions. All were handicapped by the lack of means to deal effectively with the severe problems of persons for whom the protective service agencies assumed responsibility. Even more frustrating (it would appear from the case histories), were the occasions when the available resources could not or would not respond to a client's need either because the facilities were too crowded, there was no money to pay for the service, the client did not meet eligibility requirements or for other reasons which sometimes appeared to the protective service workers to be excuses for postponing action or avoiding a difficult situation. One of the most beneficial long-range results of a protective

28

service program is that while a group of community leaders begin by examining the very specific needs of a limited group of individuals, these leaders soon find this is not enough. If the program meets with any degree of success, they end by making a critical assessment of the health and social resorces of the community and the delivery systems which are intended to bring needed services and the person needing them together.

Houston, Texas

Houston, in 1966, had a county population of approximately 1.5 million, of whom about ninety thousand or 6 percent were over sixty-five years of age, less than the national average of 9.2 percent.

A 1960 study of the older population in Houston revealed that about 20 percent were new residents. More than half of this number had moved to the city from rural areas of Texas; the rest came from other states. However, the postwar influx of younger people was so rapid that it exceeded, proportionately, the growth of the older population.

Because of the city's rapid industrial growth in the past two decades, many of the homes and commercial buildings are new. There are fast-growing suburbs with new shopping centers. In the central city, there are many new skyscrapers to accommodate business and industrial enterprises and high-rise luxury apartment buildings. Good housing facilities for middle and low-income persons are, on the other hand, quite limited, and there are only a few low-cost housing units for the elderly.

Houston is famous as a medical center. While few of the advanced medical facilities were available to the protective service program, one private hospital eventually cooperated readily, and one doctor could be counted on in emergencies. Visiting nurse service could be secured on doctor's orders, and there was a homemaker service in the community. There was a pronounced shortage of adequate institutional facilities, including homes for the aged, nursing homes and convalescent hospitals. There were no foster care homes for the aged.

A unique advantage to the protective service program in Houston was its sponsoring agency, Sheltering Arms. This is one of the few nonsectarian voluntary agencies in the entire country which serves only aged persons on a community-wide basis. It is financed primarily by the United Community Fund. Originally, it provided institutional care on a limited basis. Later the board adopted a flexible policy of intake and service in keeping with the increasing number of aged persons and their emerging new needs. The agency gradually expanded its program to provide casework and counseling, homemaker home health aide service, and a senior activities center. The agency was highly regarded in the community for its unusually active and interested citizen board of directors and its high standard of service. The board had been aware of and concerned about the increasing need of the aged persons in the community for a protective service program for some time before the NCOA project was launched. It was understandable, therefore, that the Houston program was able to get a service financed and in operation nearly a year earlier than the other demonstration.

San Diego, California

San Diego has a county population of approximately one million, of which 8.2 percent are over sixty-five. This over-65 population almost doubled between 1950 and 1960. Many newcomers were retirees who had moved from other parts of California or from the Middle West seeking a more favorable climate. Generally speaking, a larger proportion of elderly residents of San Diego were better off financially than those of many other communities, though many were living in poverty. As the program demonstrated, however, adequate financial resources are no guarantee against the need of elderly persons for protective service.

As a result of the influx of moderately well-to-do retirees, a number of new commercially sponsored apartments were built, often advertised as "retirement homes for mature adults." There was a small amount of nonprofit housing for middle income elderly. There was no public housing. Rents have risen sharply in recent years and low-cost private housing is generally unavailable to elderly persons. A small program of rent subsidy has been started. Under this federally financed program, an impoverished individual pays 25 percent of his income for rent. The difference between that amount and fair rental costs is provided by government funds.

The city has a good public geriatric hospital, a number of commercial nursing homes, foster care homes, and a visiting nurse association. Two voluntary family agencies provide a limited amount of service to elderly persons. There is no adult homemaker service except for disabled clients receiving public welfare, and no resources for home-delivered meals, except commercial firms whose prices are beyond the reach of most elderly persons. Transportation is a serious problem for many elderly persons in spite of reduced bus fares during non-rush hours.

The San Diego County Welfare Department has the advantage of California's relatively high standard of assistance payments and services for the elderly. Old Age Assistance—Old Age Security (OAS) in California—is generally adequate to meet minimal needs. Medicaid (Medical in California) provided, at the time of the project, care in nursing, convalescent and foster homes; and personal counseling. These services are available to persons who are "medically indigent." California provides for a limited guardianship service for Old Age Assistance recipients in institutions. The County Welfare Department had previously carried on a demonstration program of special services for its OAS clientele, sponsored by the American Public Welfare Association under a Ford Foundation grant. The San Diego School of Social Work provides a source of community leadership in social philosophy and practice in the field of aging.

The San Diego Protective Service program was sponsored by a new agency formed for that purpose. Whatever disadvantages lay in its lack of community recognition and stability were, in the view of many of those responsible for the program, offset by the freedom to proceed in new directions unhampered by traditional policies and regulations. The decision to form an autonomous agency with its own board of directors was made by a community-wide Advisory Committee on Protective Service, after much discussion and consideration of alternatives. The Community Council acted as fiscal agent. Federal funds were secured from the Administration on Aging in Washington under Title IV of the Older Americans Act. Part of these funds were available for a research program conducted by students at the Graduate School of Social Work at San Diego State College. Additional funds under Title III of the Older Americans Act were secured from the State of California through the Commission on Aging.

Philadelphia, Pennsylvania

Philadelphia, one of the nation's oldest and largest metropolitan areas, had a population of almost two million in 1965. The 1960 census indicated that 223,000 or 11.5 percent of the persons in the city were over 65; substantially above the national average and higher than the other two demonstration communities. Most of these older persons were long time residents concentrated in the older, poorer sections near the center of the city. Under urban renewal programs, considerable progress has been made in the downtown area in construction of commercial and public buildings. However, most of the elderly in the downtown area or peripheral sections have continued to live in dilapidated dwellings, run-down rooming houses or old hotels, as is the case in most other large cities. Philadelphia has been a leader in the development of public housing. However, in comparison to need, the number of units of public housing for the elderly, as in most other cities, is inadequate.

The city has had a long history of providing health and welfare services to its citizens and pioneered in some programs for the elderly, but it seemed unable to provide community resources adequate to the rapidly growing numbers of aged persons in the population. One sectarian voluntary agency included protection for older people as part of its total program, which reaches a limited clientele. Before the protective service program was developed, confused older people found wandering on the city streets were frequently taken to the city jail.

In 1968, the county welfare agency administered the fiscal

Old Age Assistance program, but did not provide services. A county residence for indigent elderly persons was closed for some time during the project in order to bring about certain changes in policies and standards. As the problems of many older people became more visible, an information service was established on the ground floor of city hall within a few feet of a major subway stop. In 1963, the City Department of Public Welfare* began to enlarge its services to include older people by adding a special adult service worker. Originally, services were handled by the supervisor of child welfare. Later, state funds on a 75/25 matching basis were made available to the city to allow the worker to devote full time to the identification and documentation of the service needs of the elderly. The first six months of this experience pointed to the need for specialized programs including protective service and homemaker service.

With the additional funds from the State Department of Public Welfare, it was possible for the city to establish a protective service program. Thus, the Philadelphia Department of Public Welfare through its Division of Adult Services became the sponsor of the NCOA demonstration program. As part of a public agency, the protective service program had potentially ready access to a number of city agencies, including Mental Health Services, police department, Department of Licenses and Inspection, and the mayor's and city solicitor's offices.

DEVELOPMENT OF THE DEMONSTRATION PROGRAMS

Although project objectives and general operating schemes were similar, differences among local projects became marked as soon as each demonstration began to establish services. The initial variations in approach were due to differences in administrative priorities; qualifications and characteristics of staff; availability of community resources; operational methods of

---

* This agency is to be distinguished from the County Department of Public Welfare. It provides funds for persons ineligible for the federal and state program of public assistance administered by the County Welfare agency, and for services not available elsewhere.

serving clients; and relationships with consultants, agencies, institutions and advisory groups.

In spite of these differences at the outset, it was interesting to note that certain similarities emerged as each of the projects gained experience. The knowledge acquired through successful accomplishment of protective service objectives as well as some unsuccessful attempts to resolve problems, helped to create common denominators of practice.

Houston—Focus on Use of Professional Authority

It has been noted that the sponsoring agency itself was a significant factor in the direction the protective service program in Houston took from the outset.

1. The agency itself could provide certain supportive services as they were needed.
2. The agency had established working relationships with numerous other organizations in the community, which made for easier approach to other disciplines such as law, medicine and psychiatry.
3. The agency's own intake service screened requests so that persons who appeared to need emergency service or protection were immediately assigned to the protective service staff. Thus, the project was to focus all its efforts on protective problems, while less crucial cases were handled by the agency's regular casework staff.
4. The agency board was already aware of the problems involved in protective service and was committed to the agency responsibilities involved, to the point of involuntary intervention when necessary.
5. The agency also recognized that personnel requirements went beyond those normally required of social workers, in terms of personal involvement with clients, extended and irregular hours of work, a sense of professional authority, unusual adaptability in working with representatives of other disciplines, and the willingness to accept the risks and responsibilities of acting in behalf of the client when his well-being, property or life appeared to be in jeopardy.

Budget and Staff

The budget for the program was $35,000 per year, funded by two local groups, the Moody and Fondern Foundations. The budget was admittedly low, in part because the board of directors did not want to seek federal funds until all local resources had been utilized, and in part because the agency wished to keep the budget low enough to insure that the service could be continued in the community beyond the demonstration period.

The original program called for the employment of a professionally trained and experienced project director, one trained social worker, two case aides and one clerical worker. It was planned that ample time should be spent in recruitment and training of staff and the organization of an advisory committee.

However, there were fifteen referrals during the first two weeks after the director was employed, several presenting emergency situations. The program went into immediate operation and the project director began working directly with protective service clients. It was six months before the full complement of professional staff was employed. The total staff included the director, a woman with a MSW degree and extensive experience in working with elderly persons; a young man without graduate training but with experience in public welfare and an unusual aptitude for working with disturbed elderly persons; and a part-time assistant without professional training but with several years experience in child welfare. The protective service program functioned as a unit within the agency's total program, which provided both budgetary and staff support. The protective service staff was very small to fulfill the responsibilities expected of it, but it was determined to accomplish its service goals. The project director reported at the end of the first year that "the stress of meeting severe problems with limited resources has become an advantage. The Protective Service staff has learned many time-saving techniques, and we have had to sharpen our skills. Awareness of the problem is primary. You do not make many mistakes in judgment in this type of work. If you do, you are apt to bury your mistakes."

Operational Procedures

The first policy decision made was to limit the services of the protective service project to those situations "that require special authoritative case work." These were the clients described as requiring, or potentially requiring, prompt intervention. Those cases which could be "maintained, restored or supported by traditional services" were referred to the regular casework staff of the agency. This policy decision differentiated the procedures and the philosophy of the Houston program from the other two demonstrations. "This meant," according to the project director, "that the protective service workers moved from emergency to emergency. The situations were demanding, but on the other hand, we quickly became geared to decision-making and action." Two administrative procedures were used to conserve the time of the staff, "keeping in mind the relationship between cost of caseworker time and the value of the service rendered."

One was the extensive use of the telephone. The City of Houston is larger than the State of Rhode Island and travel was a major factor in providing service. The full-time caseworker made about forty-three personal visits and 135 telephone contacts during the average working month. The staff was not sure that such extensive use of the phone was the most ideal practice, but realistically it was necessary. To make it effective, adequate trunk lines were installed and only stenographic staff capable of taking messages accurately were employed. Another procedure to supplement staff service was to secure the voluntary assistance of neighbors and friends of clients for such practical chores as shopping, taking a client to a clinic, caring for his pet if he went to a hospital or nursing home, helping with cleaning or taking in food et cetera. The staff expressed amazement at the service neighbors, landlords and even strangers would provide for a lonely, destitute person at a time of crisis. One report of the project director suggested that the ability to secure such help may depend on community attitudes and habits but went on to say that "The people of Houston, at least, still value a concern for their neighbors, and rarely is there a client who is completely without some person who, under our direction, may become quite involved in assisting him."

This type of personal help on an "as needed" basis is not the same kind of service given by volunteers organized and trained and placed by a community volunteer bureau. The protective service staff recognized that the use of neighborhood volunteers might present certain problems and they described the appropriate use of such persons as "something of an art." The staff were also aware of the potential danger that "by providing partial service, well meaning persons may help a person to maintain the status quo but prevent his getting the kind of help he really needs." On the other hand, they believed that "locating, mobilizing and supervising others so that their efforts coincide with overall casework goals can free the caseworker to use his time in direct professional relationship with the client."

Developing Community Resources and Relationships

While the new project had been announced in the community and the social, educational and health agencies had been informed of the plans for protective services, little time was devoted specifically to community publicity and interpretation. The project director's strategy was to develop community understanding and cooperation by involving individuals on a case-by-case basis. Representatives of other agencies and disciplines learned through the experience of assisting with the problems and needs of protective service clients how they could contribute to the protection of older people, and in this way new community involvements and coordinated services were developed on the practice level.

When the client was in a critical and deteriorating situation, functioning marginally, unaware of the need for or rejecting help, though in urgent need of assistance, the protective service worker was obliged to take immediate and sometimes drastic action, often necessitating medical, psychiatric or legal consultation or assistance.

As noted in the description of the community, certain resources existed in Houston for helping older people, including the preventive-supportive services of Sheltering Arms, the services of the Visiting Nurse Association and Old Age Assistance through the Public Welfare Department. Often additional services were required to meet the needs of protective service clients. Securing legal and medical help on an emergency basis presented difficult problems.

Legal consultation from private attorneys was available only to persons who had sufficient assets to pay for it. Since few protective service clients had such assets and there were no project funds for legal consultation, help was sought at first from the offices of the probate judge when involuntary intervention was needed in emergency cases.

Getting medical help for protective service clients was also a problem. Immediate medical care was frequently needed. Most physicians refused at first to make emergency house calls. Gradually, the protective service workers were able to develop medical contacts and resources. Individual physicians and other resources in clinics and hospitals became available as protective service workers persisted in their efforts to obtain the specific help needed by an individual. Cooperation and collaboration with agencies and individuals grew as the project built, case by case, a reputation for insisting on the quality, quantity and kinds of service required to protect the individual client.

Advisory Committee

As the project got underway, a technical advisory committee was gradually recruited which became an invaluable aid to the program. Its members were leaders in the professional community who could be instrumental in assisting with the more complicated problems in protection. They included the dean of a law school, the chief of gerontology in a school of medicine, the dean of a school of social work, the district director of social security, the director of public welfare, executive assistants to two probate judges, a physician, a psychiatrist and a practicing attorney.

This active committee became directly involved in resolving difficult problems and establishing policies. The members discussed in detail specific cases at committee meetings and made recommendations for action to the project director. As time went on, the committee members became very knowledgeable about protection of older people and more sophisticated about ways to obtain necessary help. Often they could provide assistance through their own agencies or smooth the way for getting help elsewhere. The Committee helped greatly to influence the community climate regarding the needs and management of elderly persons who needed protection.*

Relationship with the Courts

By working together in resolving problems case by case, the project staff and the probate court judge were able to establish an early working relationship based on mutual respect. The staff members came to be accepted as authorities in the area of protective services for the aged and were frequently consulted by the courts. Through this increased responsibility, they learned to be extremely careful in evaluation and recommendations. By the end of the first year, they were thoroughly acquainted with the law and were looked upon as trustworthy resources in cases of involuntary intervention. When court action on behalf of a protective service client appeared to be necessary, it could be arranged promptly. The workers were able, by a visit or telephone call, to discuss specific cases, and to get official opinions and support for such action as was agreed upon. This relationship between workers and courts contributed greatly to the confidence and effectiveness of the project staff.

The project's relationship with the courts proved to be helpful to the medical profession also. As a report of the project director stated, "The physician or psychiatrist in the sphere of protective services has some of the same problems as the social worker in fulfilling his professional responsibility in a strange area—that of the law. The doctor has many misunderstandings about his role as an expert in the question of incompetency and commitment to a mental hospital. He is concerned about lawsuits and is reluctant to become involved in an area in which his

---

* A fuller exposition of the activities of this committee and a transcript of a meeting at which the members discussed specific cases is included in *Overcoming Barriers to Protective Services for the Aged.* New York, NCOA Press, 1968, p. 47.

patient may lose his civil rights or be removed from his home against his will. Some doctors consider that a letter to the court recommending commitment or guardianship has the same authority as a prescription and, in effect, orders the court to take certain prescribed action. They are glad to learn that while the opinion of a family physician carries a great deal of weight with a probate judge who is struggling with a decision of competency or commitment, the judge has the final authority in this matter."

The project director found also that physicians often welcome the services of a social worker with experience in the legal aspects of protection. She cited the example of a family doctor who was completely frustrated by an elderly patient's refusal to accept medical advice for nursing home placement though she had symptoms of serious mental and physical illness. He realized that there should be court action for her protection, but he hesitated to furnish a letter to the judge because he mistakenly believed that in Texas, if a "lunacy petition" were filed, there would be no alternative except commitment to the state mental hospital. When the social worker explained that according to state law the "lunacy petition" was the legal means of removing the patient from her home and that she could be transferred to a nursing home or hospital from the psychiatric ward, the doctor was willing to provide the letter which insured his patient's admission to a psychiatric ward, from which she was soon transferred to a general hospital for medical treatment.

Professional Responsibility and Authority

As a result of the experience and knowledge gained by the staff in the day-to-day work of trying to meet the needs of severely impaired older persons in the best possible way and through the collaborative effort with other groups and individuals, a new sense of professional responsibility and authority gradually emerged. The responsibility lay in assessment of a situation in terms of the totality of social, health and legal factors involved. The professional authority lay in taking action on the basis of the assessment, which included determining, obtaining and coordinating the appropriate services to meet the client's need. Community acceptance of the protective service worker's professional authority derived from their demonstrated ability to make sound judgments and to recommend action based on understanding of available resources, legal implications and potential conflicts of interest among agencies and individuals in collaborative effort. Absorbing a remarkable amount of new information about the community and its resources was a crucial part of the protective service job of developing new methods of service delivery and demonstrating their validity.

In a situation somewhat more complicated than usual by family, health, legal and financial problems, the wide range of information and skill brought into play by the protective service worker is well illustrated.* For example, in one case, the worker needed to know about tuberculosis symptoms; public health laws; alcoholism; manifestations of mental illness; common-law marriage; postal service; social security and old age assistance regulations; guardianship; and commitment procedures. She was obliged to assess the relationships and motivations of both the divorced wife and the common-law wife, as well as the client's own strengths. It required the courage of her convictions, as well as determination and persistence with physicians, a hospital, an attorney for the common-law wife, the social security district office, the public welfare agency and the postal inspector to secure the protection needed by this man.

In commenting on the aspect of professional responsibility and authority in protective service, the project director said,

> It is essential that the social worker be effective. He must believe that 'social work is work,' and that it is a problem-solving procedure that calls for realistic results. He must be willing to use all the tools available to bring about these results. He also must be willing to exercise independent judgment and assume responsibility for his judgment. He becomes an authority figure and must assume the responsibility of that authority with full knowledge of and respect for the law. . . . Where no responsible relative is available and the impaired aged person is unaware of or unwilling to accept

---

* See Appendix II, Case Histories, Case No. VI.

the assistance to his well-being and/or safety, the necessary decisions have to be made by the protective service worker.*

Summary

The chief characteristic of the Houston project was its understanding of the use of professional authority which was instituted from the outset and developed through experience. The workers, who had had previous experience with elderly persons and their problems, tried to mobilize resources on a case-by-case basis. By demonstrating the effectiveness of intervening, when necessary, on behalf of impaired older persons, the project steadily gained the acceptance of agencies and individuals, who recognized its authoritative and coordinating role. Social, health and legal resources were brought together in a comprehensive plan of action to meet individual need in the most feasible and appropriate way.

The project's acceptance by the professional community could not have been achieved without the protective service worker's acuity in understanding and skill in social diagnosis; their knowledge of local laws and procedures regarding surrogate action, guardianship, death, autopsies, burial, wills and probate services; and their willingness to assume appropriate responsibility promptly when necessary.

The community grew to accept the protective service workers as authorities in crisis intervention, since they were able to mobilize resources and employ techniques for speedy and effective action on behalf of older persons who were in crisis or near-crisis situations. Such action was not synonymous with insitutionalization. This professional authority was sometimes used to obtain protective services for the client in a non-institutional setting in the face of some community pressures inclined to see a nursing home or a mental hospital as the obvious and perhaps permanent solution.

The medical and legal professions in particular came to accept the protective service workers as true colleagues in serving

---

* For further discussion of this subject, see *Creative Approaches in Casework with the Aging*, by Edna Wasser. New York, Family Service Association of America, 1966.

their clients' best interests. The protective service worker's assessment was frequently the deciding factor in such actions as moving a client against his will, declaration of legal competency or incompetency, preservation or deprivation of civil rights, or establishing guardianship.

It must again be noted that this summary of achievement in Houston is based on two years experience with the program.

San Diego—A New Agency With a New Program

In comparison with Houston, the development of the program in San Diego illustrated the differences in timing, administration and services when the community situation dictated the formation of a new agency.

A community-based committee on protective services made up largely of representatives of social and health agencies, spent a number of sessions considering whether one of the established health or social agencies or the community council should act as sponsor of the project. The decision was finally reached that a separate agency should be established for the demonstration, with a governing committee serving in the general capacity of board of directors (later referred to as a board).

The original group included seven members of the social work profession (mostly executives of potentially cooperating agencies); four board members of participating agencies; and eleven other individuals who represented law, medicine and psychiatry; church groups; the Mexican-American community; insurance and banking (trust department) institutions; and labor relations. (Some changes in composition were made due to resignations with the ultimate number of members being increased to thirty.) Later, a technical advisory committee was organized. There was some overlapping of members between the board and the technical advisory committee and apparently some lack of clarity as to their respective functions.

From the outset, a number of the members of the board were aware of the problems likely to be encountered. They were especially concerned that the new service should be of the highest possible standard and furnish a guide for providing protection to the community and (as part of the NCOA project) to the nation. They believed an ongoing program of protective service to be greatly needed in the community and tried to foresee ways of financing and continuing the service beyond the demonstration period. There was considerable discussion as to the distinction between continuing the *agency* and continuing the *service*. Some board members saw the board's function as giving guidance and support to a new and difficult service program in the community, regardless of the auspice under which it might operate; others saw the function more as assisting in the organization, operation and continuation of a new community agency.

At the close of official business of some board meetings, cases were presented by staff for discussion by those who wished or were able to remain and thus keep in close touch with details of program content and operation.

Staff and Staff Training

The board believed that a well-trained professional staff of several persons would be needed not only to perform an adequate service to the community but also to meet the research requirements of the San Diego State College Social Welfare Department in which twenty-one graduate students were involved and to fulfill the NCOA demonstration program commitments for record-keeping and evaluation data.

The basic staff was made up of the following: project director, MSW; worker-supervisor, MSW; two social workers, both MSW; three case aides with special experience to qualify them to relate well to older people; and two clerical workers.

Recruitment of qualified staff proved to be a severe problem due to the shortage of skilled professional social workers, the specialized and difficult nature of the duties to be performed and the noncompetitive salary scales. It was several months before the entire staff was employed, and there continued to be some fluctuations in the staff components. The general plan of operation of the program included three teams, each consisting of trained social workers and case aides.

A program of staff training was conducted in various forms throughout the project, under the direction of the senior social worker. At the beginning, there were two group meetings a week with individual conferences weekly. The curriculum included general information about elderly persons, specific characteristics of those likely to need protective service and community resources available to the program. Several community agencies participated in the training sessions, notably the County Department of Public Welfare, because of the need of many of the staff for more precise information about the financial, social service and health aspects of the county health and welfare programs. Later, training sessions revolved around problems presented by specific cases and relationships with other professional disciplines. In-service training and staff consultations continued throughout the project.

Educating the Community

The actual initiation of the program was somewhat delayed by preoccupation of staff with educating the community. Without a "ready-made status," the new protective service agency considered it essential to develop a community-wide understanding of the needs and benefits of a protective service program for older people, in order to insure acceptance and cooperation.

There was a three-pronged approach in the program of community education carried out by the project director about the nature of a protective service and the organization of a new agency. The plan was first to inform the community at large; second, to enlist the interest and collaboration of the organizations and individuals whose help would be needed by the new agency; and third, to establish relationship with potential sources of referral of clients to the agency. This program was carried out through news articles, distribution of descriptive flyers, speeches at large group meetings, conferences with agency staffs and discussions with individuals. Managers of sixty hotels with elderly residents were interviewed. The protective service film, "Rights of Age," was shown to several groups throughout the city.

An Evolving Program

A series of reports from the Project Director, over a period of approximately a year, show an interesting development relating to various aspects of the service.

At the end of the first four months, there had been fifty-one persons referred to the agency; forty-four within the final six weeks of the period. Of these, only twenty-one fell within the agency definition of need for protection. The others needed short-term counseling or help in securing some type of service, usually by referral to other agencies. Since the protective service agency was a new independent agency, it was obliged to do its own screening; a considerable amount of staff time was spent in the beginning with persons who were not actually protective service clients or even potential clients. Some agencies had earlier offered assistance in counseling; however, this assistance was not utilized. Hence, the protective service staff served all elderly persons referred to them. However, this screening process was of great value in helping the staff identify the characteristics of persons actually in need of protection.

During the first four months, therefore, no medical, psychiatric or legal consultations; no arrangements with courts or other agencies regarding conservatorship, guardianship and so forth; and no involuntary interventions were reported.

At the end of six months, the report showed substantial development in all these areas. It was reported that a firm of attorneys had volunteered their time "to consult with workers on behalf of clients with legal problems," and that "with their expert legal assistance and the cooperation of the court, involuntary conservatorships have been obtained without the need for . . . having the client declared incompetent." The report went on to say that "legal interventions are proving less difficult because they go through the Probate Court and are carefully planned wtih legal advisors" and that conservatorships had been obtained "in accordance with the plan for a protective service social worker to fill the role of Conservator of Person, while a bank or a cooperating firm of accountants served as Conservator of Estate." Voluntary conservatorships were also cited and cases in which the protective service workers had established a cooperative relationship with the client's own attorneys. In one situation, it was reported, the judge asked the counciliation court worker to consult with the protective service workers.

It was also reported that there had been progress in establishing cooperative relationships with the medical profession. "We have had the most success when we can initiate the contact with our client's physician when there is a medical problem which affects the client's living situation. Working directly with the doctor around a current situation seems to be the best public relations approach." The report goes on to say: "As we demonstrate our effectiveness and competence with specific cases, the community as a whole and the various professions with whom we are working are responding. . . . However, it is still a very slow tedious process."

The six-month report also indicates there were twenty-three cases in which the protective service worker took action on behalf of the client without his consent; all except one after consultation with an attorney, physician or psychiatrist, singly or in combination. A similar number were reported for the first quarter. There had been four cases of commitment to mental hospitals; four of guardianship; three conservatorships; and two of fiscal arrangements with guardianship.

It is perhaps significant to note here the similarities emerging in the experience of Houston and San Diego. Both show that effective relationships between protective service workers and representatatives of the three other professions essential to a total service (law, medicine and psychiatry) could be best established by working together on a case-by-case basis. Once the interdisciplinary interdependence was established through experience, the working relationship grew and flourished, as the following example cited in a San Diego report indicates:

> In the case of one client, who lived with a mentally ill daughter, the doctor showed very little concern about their living situation, their ability to take their own medication, or their ability to cook properly for themselves. The worker corresponded frequently with the doctor, giving her analysis of the home situation and seeking cooperation from the doctor in making plans for the client. However, it was not until after the client was hospitalized that the doctor turned to the protective service agency to share information and to elicit help in post hospital planning for his patient. The fact that a temporary conservatorship was obtained by the agency giving the protective service worker legal responsibility for the client, not only

made it imperative that the doctor consult with us but was, we believe, a way of giving the protective service agency status and reliability in the eyes of this physician and his colleagues.

Developing a Philosophy and Techniques of Intervention

Another similarity between Houston and San Diego was the gradual acceptance of the need, in certain situations, for a social worker to assume an authoritarian role. This does not come easy to members of a profession with a traditional attitude that the client must remain master of his own destiny.

The six-month report of the San Diego program stated the following:

> In the beginning, both individuals and other organizations believed that protective services could do all the things nobody else could—take over and move people about, make decisions for clients about their medical care, or clean up their houses. While it is true that intensive casework and imaginative use of community resources can sometimes overcome years of neglect and resistance, this intensity of effort requires tremendous amounts of staff time, while concurrently we must be doing case-finding, developing new resources and contacts, and continually evaluating what we are doing. Success in individual cases comes slowly, but often we can realize limited goals that can make a significant difference to the client.

Early reports indicated that intervention in near-crisis situations was frequently delayed. The workers proceeded slowly and cautiously when problems were complicated by the client's marginal functioning, confusion and/or resistance.

> At times, the refusal to seek medical or legal advice is the choice of the client and cannot be changed until or unless an emergency arises, despite this agency's view that medical and legal intervention is necessary for the welfare of the client. We are reluctant to take steps toward involuntary intervention unless the client is absolutely incapable of caring for himself and is in an emergency situation.
>
> In every instance, we attempt to gain the cooperation of the client before any action is taken. In several borderline cases, we have initiated action, but the degree of compliance and/or understanding is always impossible to assess. One client capitulated after some resistance and acquiesced without a real understanding of our plan.

The San Diego project was more hesitant than Houston to forego the traditional casework: emphasis on client self-determination in favor of active intervention to give the client protection. Gradually, however, the agency recognized that in certain circumstances, the client could not be appropriately helped unless the agency itself initiated intervention.

One report comments:

> The current law, which requires a doctor's statement that his patient is in danger to himself and others before an involuntary psychiatric evaluation can be made, and the reluctance of many doctors to become involved, make it difficult to obtain help for clients *unless we take court action for guardianship or conservatorship, or unless the client becomes so violent that there needs to be police intervention.**

A quotation from an unpublished paper† on the San Diego project by the senior social worker is pertinent to the development of a flexible attitude about involuntary intervention.

> The San Diego project had the advantage of being a new, free-standing agency without rules and policies which could not be changed. Both board and staff were willing to experiment, to innovate in any ways they could think of, and to take some risks which others would not.
>
> There are two sets of criteria to be considered: what is legally possible and what can be done without betraying the standards and ethics of the social work profession. Acute and constant awareness of the civil and personal rights of the individual and a dedication to preserving these must be the base from which to start. Nevertheless, if seriously impaired persons are to be given protection, some infringements of their rights of self-determination are unavoidable, and the social worker has to make peace with himself in doing what seems essential to prevent complete deterioration. It is a matter of careful judgment and not to be taken lightly to decide at what point authoritative intervention is necessary.

The paper goes on to say that:

> Prior to our taking authoritative measures, these people were

---

* In 1968 California's new Mental Health Act provided greater flexibility in conservatorship laws and protection to the "gravely disabled" without declaration of incompetence.

† Some Ethical and Procedural Problems in Providing Protective Services: A Preliminary Service Study. April 1970. Henrietta S. Misbach, ACSW, LCSW.

constantly making self-destructive decisions and refusing to recognize them as such or to accept our many offers of help in improving their situation. Passive resistance is much more common than outright refusals. On the one hand is the client who wants nothing except to be left alone in his misery, filth and starvation. On the other hand is the social worker, hesitant to interfere, to be nosey, to disregard the client's right to live as he pleases; yet fully aware that this person will soon succeed in destroying himself unless authoritative measures are applied. Who, then, can say that this individual must be given an opportunity to decide that he is able to decide? Our interventions were last-resort measures, applied only at the point that no other alternative was possible, and usually only after many efforts to persuade, cajole, and bully, in about that order of application.

Summary

San Diego's protective service program required several months of tooling up before service was started. Manpower shortages prevented immediate filling of staff positions, and an intensive program of community education was considered a prerequisite to success. Furthermore, the traditional casework philosophy of the right of an individual to determine his own destiny resulted in a cautious approach to involuntary intervention, even in crisis or near-crisis situations. However, experience indicated that postponing intervention in some cases would inevitably result in crisis. Eventually, a more flexible approach brought about significant changes in the attitude of the staff and its operational techniques.

It became obvious that a general program of community education would not automatically bring the understanding and collaboration of members of other professions essential to a protective service. Individual approaches to lawyers, doctors, psychiatrists, the courts and the trust departments of banks on a case-by-case basis proved to be the most effective method of obtaining understanding and help.

The realization that seriously impaired protective service clients were frequently incapable of making realistic decisions for their own well-being led to a new professional ethic which required the protective service worker to make decisions on their behalf for his own protection.

By the end of the first year of practice, the agency was able to report significant changes in interdisciplinary cooperation. These included appropriate referrals from the county welfare and police departments; mutual trust and coordination of services with the Visiting Nurse Association; good working relationships with mental health counselors and a geriatric hospital; acceptance by the Community Mental Health Agency of protective service workers' evaluations; observation and participation by the judge of the probate court in cases involving conservatorship; good working relationships with several law firms and numerous individual lawyers; involvement of a physician who would respond effectively in emergencies; smooth working relationships with the public administrator's office in cases of death of clients; and referrals from such sources as the Better Business Bureau, Chamber of Commerce, Social Security Administration, and City Department of Recreation.

Approaches and methods were also gradually modified to meet the protective needs of individual clients, as the workers gained confidence through experience. Arrangements were made for members of the staff to serve as guardians or conservators when there was no one else to assume this responsibility. By the end of the demonstration, a more confident approach to intervention, the development of interprofessional and interagency relationships, and better utilization of community resources greatly improved the quality of protection and assured the continuation of a protective service program in the community.

Philadelphia—Advantages and Problems of a Protective Service Program in a Public Agency

In Philadelphia, the protective service program was under the sponsorship and direction of the Philadelphia Department of Public Welfare, Division of Services for Adults. The city agency provides financial and other help to Philadelphia citizens who are not eligible for public welfare assistance programs. It is primarily a service agency.

The Division on Services for Adults in the Philadelphia Department of Public Welfare was organized in 1966. In 1967, when the protective service program was inaugurated, the agency served primarily as a centralized resource for screening, counseling and referral, including assistance in nursing or boarding home placement. A homemaker service was inaugurated in March 1967. The plan for a protective service program was developed the same year. Funding of the protective service program was on a 90 to 10 percent sharing basis by the Pennsylvania State Department of Public Welfare and the City of Philadelphia. The staff for the Division of Adult Services included a director, a legal consultant, a supervisor, five social workers, a social work trainee and six homemakers.

Staff

The director of the Adult Services Division, a worker with an MSW degree, was also named director of the Protective Service Project. Since he was not relieved of any other responsibilities, obviously he could give only part time to supervising the protective service program and very little time to direct service. However, he frequently became involved in the most critical cases, assisting with direct services and expediting action by other agencies, institutions or individuals.

One of the director's major administrative priorities was to employ qualified staff. All staff positions were covered by civil service regulations, a situation which presented serious problems. The regulations required that workers should have a bachelor's degree. There were no specifications for professional social work training, experience or personal characteristics indicating a worker's ability to relate easily to and work with the elderly. The salary scale was not high enough to attract experienced social workers or those with advanced degrees. Despite intensive recruitment efforts, it was impossible to secure workers with the combination of temperament, training and experience recommended by NCOA. Consequently, two persons employed as social workers by the Adult Services Division were "assigned" to the protective service program, and there was considerable turnover. Altogether, 1,385 elderly persons were served by the Adult Service Division during the year of the demonstration, 140 of whom were considered by definition to be protective service clients. It appears obvious that the two protective service workers had much too large a case load to handle adequately, especially in view of the large number of requests for emergency help.

It should be pointed out that the protective service program was not widely recognized in the agency as a "demonstration" which might be entitled to some priority in staff assignment; rather, it was regarded as the initial phase of one other new service being added to the agency's total program. This attitude, however, turned out to have an important positive value in that the program was viewed from the beginning as permanent. For this reason, there may have been less feeling of urgency to make as much progress as possible during the first year. It was also important not to conduct the program on a scale which would preclude its continuation.

Utilizing Community Resources

In view of the administrative problems of securing qualified personnel, staff turnover and the growing number of requests for help, the director increased his efforts to develop a roster of medical and legal consultants and to obtain active cooperation from agencies and institutions, especially in the public sector, which could give supportive services. These resources were being severely taxed at this time, owing to the fact that the State Department of Public Welfare had recently closed new admissions to the city's large custodial facility; and that after reorganization, admissions of elderly persons to the facility were limited to the physically well.

Initial cooperating community resources identified by the director were Community Nursing Service; Police Department; Protective Service Advisory Committee; Philadelphia County Board of Assistance (a state agency); City Department of Licenses and Inspections; Philadelphia General Hospital; Traveler's Aid Society; the City Division of Mental Health; the Health and Welfare Council; the Philadelphia Housing Authority; and the Mayor's Advisory Committee on Aging.

Advisory Committee

Before the protective service program was inaugurated, there had been a citywide Technical Committee on Protective Services. During the year, the Committee was reorganized as the Advisory Committee on Protective Services to the Aging. The purpose for the change, according to the director, was to enable recruitment of a cross section of influential members of the community who had expressed interest in the health and welfare of the aging rather than to limit membership to those who were qualified by reasons of professional training.

At its initial meetings, the Committee attempted to identify the kinds of resources required for a complete protective service, which might be lacking in the community. They questioned the adequacy of nursing home facilities and discussed the need for a temporary adult shelter to prevent the use of the county jail to lodge elderly persons found wandering in the streets by police; a facility for the chronically ill aged; and a comprehensive physical and mental health program for the aged.

It was suggested that one of the important functions of the protective service program would be to document these needs. The group recognized the need for legislation which would permit the appointment of public guardians in each county. In the meantime, they offered to develop a "pool" of twelve volunteers who would be willing to act as guardians. Other subjects of interest to the advisory committee were the relationship of the case load to the agency's ability to expand and handling the public information aspects of the program in such a way as to keep the demand for and supply of protective services in some reasonable balance. There is nothing in the minutes or reports of the advisory committee's work to indicate that its members were ever concerned with methods of handling individual cases, though individual members undoubtedly were made aware of the kinds of situations which made protection necessary.

Committees were appointed to work out details of action in those areas for which responsibility was accepted. For example, the advisory committee was largely instrumental in securing psychiatric evaluations in emergency situations by the mental health centers.

Providing Service

Because of the location of the program in an agency which provided certain direct services and which invited requests for help of many kinds from older persons with varying degrees of need, the understanding of protective service was somewhat blurred. The line between supportive and surrogate service was particularly difficult to draw. The director wrote in an early report:

> Those requiring protective service have been seen in many varied forms, making it difficult to arrive at a single, clear, concise definition of 'degrees of intervention.' The public is quick to verbalize its overwhelming desire for extension of this service, especially at the point of crisis, but almost always it is presumed that the Department has the authority or legal sanction to act in behalf of aged adults in need of protection who do not agree to be served. Many of the specific requests for this service from relatives, friends and neighbors, range from 'clean up that filthy house next door to me' or 'put him away; he should not be let loose in the community.'*
>
> . . . .
>
> . . . activity on behalf of elderly persons occasionally raises questions of privacy, intervention, and legal sanctions." [Because of the considerable degree of legal involvement in protective service, Division personnel worked very closely with its legal consultant.]
>
> Emergency psychiatric examinations are provided for aged persons who are without available relatives or friends to initiate action. When it was established that 'danger' was imminent and no other resource was available within the community to assist, the Division, with the advice of the Legal Consultant, secured a Court order in accordance with the Mental Health Act and followed through with placement of the client in the appropriate mental health facility, assuring appropriate follow-up. There has been some question about the advisability of this Division functioning in such a role. However, six persons were served in this way during 1967.

Relationship With Other Public Agencies

One of the obvious advantages of locating a program in a public service agency is the ready access it presumably provides

---

* A common assumption is that a public agency has greater legal authority to intervene in a surrogate function than private agencies, simply because it is public. The opposite is true. The general legal rule is that a local public agency can do only those things specifically authorized by statute; that is, if statute does not say specifically that an agency can't, and doesn't say it can, then it can't. This is reverse of rule which generally applies to private agencies.

to services of other departments of government. This may not always work as simply as is generally supposed. There were certain problems involved in the effort to coordinate the multiplicity of public agencies, each with its own authority and jurisdictional limitation, and it was often necessary for the protective service workers to exercise firm leadership.

One example of the double aspects of these relationships is evident in the recurring problem of elderly persons living in unsafe housing. When older persons were found living in surroundings which had become health hazards to themselves and their neighbors, referral was usually made to the City Department of Licenses and Inspections. In many such cases, action was delayed or not taken. In others, more than one city agency might be involved at the same time. The following extract from a case record gives an example of these problems:

> When neighbors complained about the living conditions of Mr. Smith, who was in his late 70's, a protective service worker visited him. Mr. Smith talked with her but did not let her into the house. The worker, who was inexperienced in recognizing serious symptoms, reported that he seemed to be in good health. After a series of further complaints from neighbors over a period of months, a second worker visited. When no one answered the door, the worker looked through the window and saw refuse and garbage piled high inside. After numerous calls to the city department responsible for housing inspection, action was finally taken; the house was condemned and posted as 'unfit for human habitation,' and the heat, electricity, and water were turned off. Mr. Smith, however, continued to live there for several months in a confused state.
>
> The protective service worker, on advice of legal counsel, attempted to find someone who would serve as guardian. After such a person was finally located, it was discovered that the neighbors, in the meantime, had called the mental health center. A psychiatrist made a home call, and as a result, Mr. Smith was hospitalized. When the protective service worker became doubtful about the reliability of the prospective guardian, the city solicitor, who was acting as legal advisor to the protective service program, recommended that the case be closed insofar as protective services were concerned, since the responsibility could now be assumed by another agency.

Problems and Progress

The program's frequent staff turnover and heavy case loads made it impossible for the staff to keep up with all the records required for analysis by the NCOA protective service project. A brief statistical record was prepared, and NCOA's project director conducted extensive interviews with workers assigned to protective service cases and with persons from other agencies who worked with the elderly. Two-thirds of the narrative case records of protective service clients were reviewed.

The records revealed that those clients whose problems were least complicated or those whose needs had had direct attention from the director of the project had usually received protective services appropriate to their needs. In numerous other cases, the problems were too difficult or "too time consuming" for the staff to handle promptly.

Situations such as the following were typical of those confronting the protective service workers:

> Many older persons who lived alone were increasingly unable to manage in dilapidated and dangerous living quarters. Safe, low-cost housing was unavailable. Some persons, classified as 'vagrants' by the police, refused to go to the city's custodial home for older people and were temporarily lodged in jail, and when they were released, the problem began all over again.
>
> Large numbers of aged individuals or couples had serious health problems as well as poor living arrangements. The visiting nurses frequently referred these persons for protective services and possible placement in hospitals or nursing homes. If a client refused help and homemakers became unwilling to clean up the filth, no help was available until an accident or other crisis precipitated action. In numerous instances in which the worker finally persuaded the client to enter a hospital or nursing home, there were no beds or accommodations available, and frequently the clients' condition became critical before arrangements for care and treatment could be made.

The records indicated that the protective service workers were frequently unable to visit clients except in emergency situations or unless the requests came from sources demanding prompt action. Depending on the degree of urgency, a case was "investigated," sometimes only by telephone.

When the situation was complicated by the client's confusion and/or rejection of the worker, the "investigation" might continue over a period of weeks or months, during which time the worker, with many other demands on his time, would attempt to resolve the problem by finding better housing, getting a psychiatric evaluation, locating a guardian, obtaining legal sanction for involuntary intervention, placing the client in a nursing home, or convincing another agency to assist with the problem.

In spite of difficulties and obstacles, the protective service program in Philadelphia at the end of its first year showed marked achievement and great promise. There were instances in which exploitation of an older person was halted when a protective service worker became involved in the case. For example, if the worker could verify the information that an elderly individual was being overcharged for inadequate housing or medical care, it was possible for him to see that corrective action was taken, often in cooperation with other agencies.

Other examples of improvement in services included the use of temporary custody court petitions to obtain medical and psychiatric observation at mental health centers; extension of homemaker and foster care services within the Adult Services Division; greater cooperation with other city and county public agencies, hospitals and nursing homes. The protective service workers were becoming accepted as "coordinators of services" in bringing protection to the aged.

At the end of the year, the Division on Aging was granted funds for salary increases and additional staff positions. The director indicated that "the major problems needing priority attention during the second year were selection of staff members who would relate to and work well with older people; in-service training on understanding old people's problems and protecting their rights, well-being and property; and legal consultation readily accessible to all staff members."

Summary

The protective service program in Philadelphia shared many of the problems and much of the progress experienced by the other two programs during the first year. It had additional drawbacks, as well as advantages, owing to its location in a public agency. There was less freedom in staff selection because of civil service regulations, which included salary limitations. As a result, staff qualifications were lower than outlined in the NCOA recommendations. On the other hand, there was easier access to public facilities and—to a degree—legal services.

In order to take advantage of these public facilities, the protective service staff had to build up professional relationships and demonstrate the value of team effort in solving serious problems of impaired elderly people. Since many of the cooperating agencies operated under legal mandate, the final decision for management of client's affairs did not always rest with the protective service program.

By the end of the first year, substantial progress has been made toward establishing cooperative relationship with a multiplicity of agencies and there was wide recognition of the protective service staff's experience, commitment, energy and effort—all of which are essential to effective protective service. With an increased budget and staff, substantial improvement in the program could be anticipated for the future.

SIMILARITIES AND DIFFERENCES AMONG THE THREE PROGRAMS

The director of NCOA's project on protective services maintained close contact with each of the demonstration programs, giving assistance wherever possible in overcoming the problems of organizing and providing the service.

When the evaluation was instituted, the three local programs were in three different stages of development. Two were still in initial stages of organization. One was just beginning practice, with shortages of personnel; the other was tooling up, but had not yet begun direct service. The third had already completed one year of operation and had accumulated enough experience to develop a sound program of services and gain acceptance throughout the community.

Evaluation schedules were requested from each of the programs. The evaluator was particularly struck with the basic similarity of the experience in the three communities in the development stage. Differences in accomplishment of the objectives appeared to be due in part, at least, to the length of time the program had been in operation.

It was apparent that in developing a protective service program, the first year was bound to be fraught with misgiving, frustration and failure to achieve established goals. By the end of a year, it was possible to identify the essentials of effective service, qualified staff, good working relationships with a multiplicity of agencies, access to certain basic supportive services, better understanding of impaired old people and improved techniques of diagnosis and intervention. In each of the demonstration programs, substantial progress in all these areas could be documented.

Chapter IV

Protective Service Clients

I<small>N THE THREE</small> demonstration programs, a total of 330 individuals were served during the year 1967 when the evaluation records were kept. Based on a twenty-page multiple choice schedule, personal characteristics, needs, services and progress were recorded on each client, with the exceptions noted in the previous chapters. This chapter on client characteristics and the following chapter on services are based in large part on material selected from these records.*

In Houston, the number of persons on which evaluation records were kept was 121; in San Diego, 118; and in Philadelphia, 91. It is not possible to suggest from the figures how many other elderly persons in the community were in need of protection; nor did the projects provide a basis for projecting a percentage of persons over sixty-five who might be considered in need of protective service. (Unverified estimates have suggested from 5 percent to more than 10 percent of all persons over sixty-five.) There was an interesting relationship between the number who sought the services of the agency or were referred to it and the number considered by the staff to be protective service clients.

In Houston, 1184 elderly persons applied or were referred to Sheltering Arms for counseling or special services. Roughly, 10 percent of these were referred in the screening process to the protective service program. In Philadelphia, the City Department of Public Welfare recorded 1385 counseling cases which had been

---

* It is not possible to include here all the tables or to summarize all the information obtained. More detailed data and analysis in some specific areas may be secured from the office of the National Council on the Aging, 1828 "L" Street, N.W., Washington, D.C. 20036.

referred for services.* Nearly 7 percent were considered as falling under the NCOA definition of protective service clients. In San Diego, 2800 persons receiving Old Age Assistance were considered "service cases." Only persons considered to be in need of protective service were referred to the demonstration program. Of the 223 referrals, about half were accepted as in need of protection.

CLIENT CHARACTERISTICS

Age

As will be noted from the following table, most of the protective service clients were in the upper age brackets at intake. Of the entire group of 330 persons in the three programs, 243 were over seventy years of age. Of these, 130 were over eighty; 25 were over ninety; and about one-fourth were under seventy.

TABLE I

AGE OF CLIENT

Age in Initial Period	Houston No.	%	Philadelphia No.	%	San Diego No.	%
Total	121	100.0	91	100.0	118	100.0
Under 60 years	0	0.0	8	8.8	2	1.7
60 through 64 years	10	8.3	5	5.5	7	5.9
65 through 69 years	22	18.2	11	21.1	17	14.4
70 through 74 years	27	22.3	19	20.9	19	16.1
75 through 79 years	18	14.9	14	15.4	16	13.6
80 through 84 years	20	16.5	18	19.8	30	25.4
85 through 89 years	19	14.9	7	7.7	12	10.2
90 through 94 years	4	3.3	1	1.1	7	5.9
95 years and over	1	0.8	8	8.8	4	3.4
Not reported	1	0.8			4	3.4

Sex and Race

There were more women than men: 63 percent in Houston; 56 percent in Philadelphia; and 70 percent in San Diego. More than three-fourths were white. However, a higher proportion of Negroes were served than their ratio in the communities. In Houston, 25.6 percent of the protective service clients were

---

* In Philadelphia, the city agency was the only public agency which offered this service but few cases were referred from the County Public Assistance (OAA).

Negroes as compared with 16 percent Negro population in the community. In Philadelphia, the respective figures were 25 percent and 17 percent; in San Diego, 11 percent and 3 percent.

Marital Status and Household Composition

Data on these and some other categories were not recorded in Philadelphia. The significant figures in Table II show that in both Houston and San Diego, only 10 percent of the protective service clients were married with spouse present and that about 60 percent were widowed. Table III indicates that about half were living alone. It should be noted the household composition showed little variation by city except that about one-fifth of Houston clients were living in institutions or other group living arrangements at the time of intake as compared with 6.8 percent in San Diego.

TABLE II
MARITAL STATUS

Marital Status	Houston No.	%	San Diego No.	%
Total	121	100.0	118	100.0
Married, spouse present	13	10.7	12	10.2
Married, spouse absent	3	2.5	6	5.1
Widowed	73	60.3	70	59.3
Separated	1	0.8	0	0.0
Divorced	17	14.1	5	4.2
Never married	8	6.6	20	16.9
Not married, but living with friend of opposite sex	0	0.0	4	3.4
Indeterminate	6	5.0	1	0.9

TABLE III
HOUSEHOLD COMPOSITION

Living Arrangement	Houston No.	%	San Diego No.	%
Total	121	100.0	118	100.0
Client living alone	59	48.8	65	55.1
Client living with spouse only	9	7.4	8	6.8
Client living with spouse and others	4	3.3	3	2.5
Client living with other related persons	15	12.4	17	14.4
Client living with nonrelated persons	7	5.8	13	11.9
Client living in group quarters or institution	25	20.7	8	6.8
Other	2	1.6	4	3.4

Income and Assets

Of the total number of 330 on whom records were kept (58 in Houston, 31 in Philadelphia, and 30 in San Diego), 119 reported less than $100 per month income. Only 40 (10 in Houston, 6 in Philadelphia, and 24 in San Diego) reported incomes of $200 and over per month.

TABLE IV

INCOME OF CLIENT'S HOUSEHOLD

Income Bracket (Monthly)	Houston No.	%	Philadelphia No.	%	San Diego No.	%
Total	121	100.0	91	100.0	118	100.0
Less than $49	13	10.8	11	12.1	9	7.6
$50 through $99	45	37.2	20	22.0	21	17.8
$100 through $149	36	29.7	0	0	16	13.5
$150 through $199	14	11.6	22	24.2	19	16.1
$200 through $299	7	5.8	5	5.5	14	11.9
$300 and over	3	2.5	1	1.1	10	8.5
Indeterminate	3	2.5	32	35.2	26	22.0
Not reported	0	0.0	0	0.0	3	2.5

In Houston, nearly four-fifths derived most of their income from Social Security, Old Age Assistance, or a combination of the two. In San Diego, 35 percent derived most of their income from Social Security and 46 percent derived most of it from other pensions, interests and use of capital.

Less than half of those in San Diego and less than a third in Houston owned their own homes. In San Diego, 13.5 percent of the homeowners had homes assessed at more than $10,000 and 11 percent at less than $5,000. In Houston, 4 percent of the homes owned by clients were assessed at more than $10,000 and 12 percent at under $5,000. Aside from home ownership, 55 percent in Houston reported no other assets and 4 percent reported other assets over $15,000. In San Diego, the comparable figures were 18 percent with no other assets and 12 percent with more than $15,000. The relatively higher economic status of the San Diego clients is indicative that poverty is by no means the only decisive factor in the need of elderly persons for protective service.

Housing and Living Conditions

In both Houston and San Diego, over half the protective service clients were living in a single family house or duplex;

about 18 percent lived in apartments; 5 percent of these in Houston and 9 percent in San Diego lived in single rooms.

The condition of housing was rated in three categories:

Sound housing was defined as "that which has no defects, or only slight defects which normally are corrected during the course of regular maintenance."

Deteriorating housing was defined as that which "needs more repair than would be provided in the course of regular maintenance. It has one or more defects of an intermediate nature that must be corrected if the unit is to continue to provide safe and adequate housing."

Dilapidated housing was that which "does not provide safe and adequate shelter and in its present condition endangers the health, safety or well-being of the occupants."

Omitting those in institutional housing, a little more than half of the Houston clients lived in sound housing and a little less than half in deteriorated or dilapidated. In San Diego, the comparative figures were two-thirds and one-third.

Quality of living conditions within the house was measured on the basis of the following factors: heat, light, space and adequacy of furnishings; cleanliness was assessed in terms of absence of filth and litter. Of the 121 clients in Houston, 30 were judged to have "good" living conditions and 34 "very poor." Of the 118 clients in San Diego, 55 were judged to have "good" living conditions and 17 "very poor."

Regardless of its condition, the costs of housing in relation to income were high for many clients. In Houston, 22 percent paid from one-third to one-half of their income for shelter and 7 percent paid over one-half of income. In San Diego, where rents were somewhat higher, corresponding figures were 34 percent and 18 percent.

Mobility and Physical Competence

These factors have an important bearing on the nature and extent of need as well as on methods of working out solutions for elderly persons in need of protection. As will be seen in Table V below, 19 clients in Houston were bedridden; 46 more were housebound; 38 could get to the porch or neighborhood;

only 1 percent could use public transportation or drive a car.

In San Diego, 3 were bedridden; 28 more were housebound; 46 could get to the porch or neighborhood; 35 could use public transportation or drive a car.

TABLE V

RELATIVE MOBILITY OF CLIENT AT INITIAL CONTACT

	Houston		San Diego	
Extent of Mobility	*No.*	*%*	*No.*	*%*
Total	121	100.0	118	100.0
Bedridden	19	15.7	3	2.5
Partially bedridden (in bed part day of week)	15	12.4	13	11.0
Confined to wheelchair and housebound	14	11.6	6	5.1
Housebound (unable to go outside)	17	14.1	9	7.6
Able to get to nearby outdoors (yard or porch)	20	16.5	21	17.8
Able to get into neighborhood	18	14.9	25	21.2
Able to take public transportation with help	1	0.8	6	5.1
Able to take public transportation alone	14	11.6	24	20.3
Able to drive a car safely	2	1.6	3	2.5
Client drives car (despite danger to self and others)	0	0.0	2	1.7
Other	1	0.8	6	5.1

Another measure of physical competence was the ability of individuals to perform eleven specified tasks. These were:

1. Feeds self
2. Bathes independently
3. Dresses independently
4. Independent toileting
5. Moves out of bed independently
6. Does own light housework (makes own bed, keeps house in good order)
7. Walks at least one flight of stairs
8. Able to walk outdoors
9. Does own cooking
10. Does own local shopping
11. Does heavy household cleaning (washes clothes, cleans windows, scrubs)

Ability to perform these tasks was rated on a point basis. The scores showed severe physical impairments in 54 percent of the Houston clients; moderate impairment in 27 percent; mild impairment in 19 percent. In San Diego, 16 percent showed severe impairment; 50 percent moderate impairment; and 43 percent mild impairment.

The high proportion of severely impaired and housebound clients in Houston is evident. In its second year of operation, the Houston program reached an even greater number of persons gravely disabled and in need of immediate protection. Their condition frequently required a move to protective environments such as institutions or other congregate living arrangements.

Mood and Behavior

These characteristics were judged at the end of the first month of contact. Six indicators of affective disorder were considered: generalized anxiety; psychosis (hallucinations, delusions, inability to distinguish fantasy from reality); paranoid trends (unwarranted suspiciousness); depression; generalized anger; and drug or alcoholic addiction.

About three-fourths of the Houston group were judged to have a great deal of generalized anxiety; about one-fourth were judged to be psychotic; 44 percent showed marked paranoid trends; and 67 percent were seriously depressed. Addiction to either alcohol or drugs was minimal.

In the San Diego group, 39 percent were considered to have generalized anxiety to a substantial degree; one-third were judged to be seriously depressed or to have paranoid trends; 6 percent were judged to be psychotic. A small proportion were addicted to drugs or alcohol.

Seven indicators of behavioral disorder were considered. Protective service workers in Houston and San Diego scored the list of troublesome behavior manifestations on a four-point scale from "dangerous" to "none." Those characteristics which were rated dangerous or severe were ranked and are reported in Table VI below.

TABLE VI

BEHAVIOR ATTRIBUTE OR MANIFESTATION

	Houston		San Diego	
	%	Rank	%	Rank
Poor judgment in self-care and hygiene	70.2	1	20.5	3
Poor health habits (insomnia, failure to use doctor or medication)	69.4	2	37.2	1
Poor judgment in eating habits	59.5	3	28.0	4
Poor judgment in using funds (hoarding or extravagance)	52.1	4	30.5	2
Interpersonal disturbances (disordered behavior toward others, argumentative)	47.9	5	21.1	5
Confusion (wandering; getting lost, etc.)	45.4	6	7.8	6
Offensive social behavior (drunkenness, exhibitionism, law violation, etc.)	24.0	7	6.7	7

It will be noted that the top four behavioral programs are the same in both cities, though the rank order is different.

A number of undesirable behavioral attributes relate to personal health practices. This suggests the probability of a high positive association between emotional or mental incapacity and poor health. One can only speculate on the extent to which the poor health practices contribute to the poor mental state or the negative effects of emotional, social or disoriented mental conditions contribute to poor physical health.

Summary

It seems clear from the records and ratings that of persons served or in need of protection tend to be older, poorer, less mobile than the rest of the elderly population; to have serious difficulties in performance of tasks of daily living; to suffer certain affective and behavioral disorders; and to be without the normal supports of spouse, family and friends.

At the same time, the danger of generalization becomes quite clear. It must be noted that none of the characteristics listed above can be applied to all persons in need of protection. Some are relatively young; some have no financial problems, do not exhibit offensive social behavior, are mobile and do not wander or show poor judgment in use of funds or in self-care. Protective service clients, far from being a "category," are perhaps the most individual of elderly persons.

REFERRAL OF CLIENTS

In the light of the characteristics summarized above, it is interesting to note the extent to which they were reflected in the sources of and the reasons for referral of clients to the protective service programs.

Sources of Referral

The very wide range of sources of referral in all three communities can be seen in the following table:

TABLE VII

SOURCES OF REFERRAL

Sources of Referral	Houston		Philadelphia		San Diego	
	No.	%	No.	%	No.	%
Total	121	100.0	91	100.0	118	100.0
Friend and neighbor	19	15.7	15	16.5	15	12.6
Public welfare department	19	15.7	9	9.9	22	18.6
Relative	14	11.6	9	9.9	7	5.9
Nurse of public or voluntary agency	13	10.7	4	4.4	17	14.5
Hospital or nursing home	6	5.0	10	11.0	7	5.9
Attorney	0	0.0	1	1.1	4	3.4
Physician in private practice	11	9.1	0	0.0	1	0.9
Courts	7	5.8	0	0.0	1	0.9
Client self-referral	12	9.9	2	2.2	6	5.1
Project case finder or worker	4	3.3	0	0.0	2	2.5
Information referral service	3	2.5	1	1.1	3	2.5
Voluntary casework agency	1	0.8	1	1.1	6	5.1
Clergy	3	2.5	2	2.2	3	2.5
Landlord (private housing)	2	1.6	5	5.5	5	4.2
Psychiatrist in private practice	0	0.0	0	0.0	1	0.9
Other	7	5.8	32*	35.2	17†	14.5

Reasons for Referral

It is significant that the referral sources and the protective service staff in both Houston and San Diego were in general agreement that the most frequent client problems which led to the need for protective services were (a) inadequate self-care conceived of as incapacity to carry out tasks for daily living; (b) danger to self because of neglect of personal needs, mal-

* "Other" identified in Philadelphia as including House of Corrections, Social Security Office, State Office of Aging, OEO Office, Senior Citizens Club, City Office of Licensing and Inspection (Sanitation), mayor's office, police, Public Housing, former employer.

† "Other" identified in San Diego as including bank officer and senior citizen programs.

nutrition, confusion or alcoholism; and (c) unmanageable circumstances of physical environment.

All agreed that the largest number of problems fell in the first category. The referral sources and the project workers disagreed on the rank of numbers 2 and 3 as indicated in Table VIII.

TABLE VIII

REASONS FOR NEED OF PROTECTIVE SERVICE AS IDENTIFIED
BY REFERRAL SOURCE AND PROJECT STAFF

Nature of Protective Problem	Houston Reference Source	Houston Project Worker	%	San Diego Reference Source	San Diego Project Worker	%
Total	121*	121	100.0	118	118	100.0
Inadequate self-care: incapacity in daily living	62	42	34.7	40	47	39.8
Danger to self: indirect (neglect, confusion, alcoholism, etc.)	13	28	23.1	14	20	16.9
Unmanageable physical environmental circumstances	17	13	10.7	17	10	8.5
Interpersonal conflicts; conduct disturbing, worrisome	7	13	10.7	7	10	8.5
Defective decision-making: other than financial	9	10	1.6	12	11	9.3
Defective decision-making: financial matters	5	1	0.8	11	8	6.8
Danger to others: direct (aggressive, assaultive)	4	6	5.0	1	2	1.7
Exploitation (actual or potential)	1	3	2.5	9	3	2.5
Conflict with community: conduct offensive, obnoxious, unlawful	3	1	0.8	5	2	1.7
Danger to self: direct (conscious self-aggression)	1	2	1.6	1	0	0.0
Danger to others: indirect (confusion, carelessness, etc.)	4	1	0.8	0	1	0.9
Indeterminate	1	1	0.8	1	4	3.4

* More than one problem was designated for a few of Houston's cases, resulting in a total of 127 problems for 121 cases. Percentages, however, are related to the total of 121 cases. This results in a slight distortion when comparing the experience of Houston with that of San Diego.

CLASSIFICATION SYSTEM

One of the problems of determining the appropriate action to be taken in relation to clients has been the lack of clarity about the various factors which influence the decision. Beyond some broad descriptions of those apt to be in need of help, no attempt has been made to record the nature and degree of incompetence and the relationship between environmental factors and incompetency.

One of the important parts of the research efforts in the demonstration programs was to formulate and try out a simple classification system based on functional ability and environmental circumstances which would give a workable profile of the protective service client. The type of service given and the effectiveness of its outcome would depend on an interplay of these two factors. For example, a severely impaired person might continue a relatively safe existence if there were persons to see that his personal needs were cared for and if he had satisfactory housing. If he did not have these supports, he might well need protective services.

The classification system devised was used as a guide for the staff in identifying the crucial elements in the total situation of the client, a tool in determining the nature of the service needed and a measure of the effectiveness of the service given.

The classification system is recognized as only a beginning attempt to relate ability to function and environmental safety. It is the belief of NCOA and the protective service workers, however, that it served as a useful guide to evaluation and service.

Functional Classifications

Four levels of ability to function were defined and illustrated as follows:

Self-determining (Potential Protective Service Case)

This individual is mentally capable of caring for himself and his interests; able to maintain at least minimal social standards of self-care and conduct, despite a few or occasional signs of mental disorder or malfunction, but may be in need of some counseling and perhaps referral for service although he is able to make his own arrangements for whatever help he needs. After initial contact, a recommendation might be made for annual or semi-annual review but an individual would not be considered a protective service client at the time of the first interview, unless his environmental classification was "unsafe."

An 80-year-old man has a 62-year-old wife who is dull normal in intellect. He is concerned that she will be exploited after his death, yet she is not actually incompetent nor is there sufficient property to justify an expensive guardianship. As there is no other person or agency concerned, this case would be reviewed periodically in order to prevent crisis in case of serious illness or death of spouse.

An 86-year-old woman is quite helpless from arthritis. She is mentally alert, cooperative and a very gregarious person. Her children, living in a distant city, are concerned and have requested the agency's assistance in planning for their parent. Plans for improving her living arrangements are made by the caseworker in consultation with her. This is only a potential protective service case even though the client calls the caseworker in lieu of her family for help and advice when she feels she needs it. However, if her physical condition should create an emergency, and the children were not available, it might be that the agency would have to serve in a protective service capacity to meet her needs. In the meantime, the agency takes no action except in response to requests.

Marginally Competent

This individual is only partially capable of adequately caring for himself and his interests and is able to maintain only minimal or intermittent levels of social functioning (self-care and conduct) by reason of mental disorder or malfunction. The degree of severity or regularity of mental disorder distinguishes the marginally competent from the incompetent.

A woman, aged 80, was referred by the Visiting Nurse Service to protective service. She suffered from diabetes and was intermittently confused and disoriented but unwilling to accept care. She was capable of handling funds but had an obsession about not spending money for even a minimum standard of health and comfort.

A brother and sister were both mentally disturbed. The sister refused to allow her brother to have medical care or to cooperate with any reasonable plan for him. He became quite ill and was committed to a mental hospital. The sister traveled alone to Washington to report this action to the committee for protection of constitutional rights.

Incompetent

This person is mentally incapable of adequately caring for himself and his interests. He is unable to maintain minimal social standards of self-care and conduct by reason of mental disorder or malfunction, manifested by serious disturbances or abnormalities of thought, feeling and behavior, which may be due to either physical or psychological causes such as organic brain damage, neurosis, temporary or chronic illness, or lifelong mental retardation. The mental disorder or malfunction may be manifested by confused thinking and poor judgment, by extreme expressions of emotion, or by bizarre, asocial or harmful behavior. (A physical disorder or infirmity may cause, accompany or exacerbate the mental malfunctioning of the aged. However, a physical disorder or infirmity alone does not classify a person as needing protection for the purposes of this study unless it affects mental functioning, for example, malnutrition.)

> A man, aged eighty-three, refused to leave his home which had been condemned by city officials as "unfit for human habitation." Despite severe illness, he refused to go to a hospital. One thousand dollars worth of uncashed Social Security checks were found in the house.

Dangerously Incompetent

This person is in immediate crisis without help; there is likelihood of serious injury or death to himself or others. He is too ill to differentiate between reality and unreality. Action in such cases, whether accepted or not by the client, cannot be postponed.

> A woman living alone refused to have a doctor, although a leg infection had become so critical that without immediate medical help, she would likely die. Her house was in complete disorder and her several cats were obviously starving. She was sure the patent medicine she was taking would make her well.
>
> A woman of Italian descent had never integrated into American culture. She had one daughter whom she deserted when the child was very young. When she was referred to the agency, she had been living as a recluse, surrounded by unhousebroken cats and filth. The precipitating factor of referral was her uncontrolled hostility toward the neighborhood children, frequently throwing boiling water on them when they were playing outside her window. After several children were hurt, the case was reported to the authorities who referred her to the agency.
>
> A woman, aged seventy-six, and her 81-year-old husband lived in a public housing project. She was malnourished and confused. The apartment was very disorganized as evidenced by scattered dirty clothes and debris and by old feces and urine stains on the

floor. She cannot recall when she last ate or where the kitchen is located. When visited, she initiated no verbal communications, nor was she coherent in her responses. Her husband appeared to be suffering from a high fever and was delirious.

Among the 330 protective service clients classified in the demonstration programs, 65 were considered self-determining at the time of first interview; 135, marginally competent; 86, incompetent; and 37, dangerously incompetent, with 7, indeterminate. It is interesting to note (see Table IX) that the greatest variation in the three cities is in the proportion of cases classified as "dangerously incompetent." One-fourth of the cases in Houston were in this category, but only 4 percent in San Diego, and 2 percent in Philadelphia. This may reflect the situation referred to previously, namely that the Houston report was based on a second year of experience reflecting a greater sophistication in dealing with difficult situations, more extensive case findings and a greater number of referrals of persons in or near crisis.

Environmental Classifications

It is to be noted that in judging an environmental situation, both physical and social factors were considered. Criteria included safety, sanitation, decency, health and comfort.

Four degrees of environmental support, social and physical, were identified.

Manageable

The environment can provide the basic living supports necessary for the client.

> An elderly physically frail woman lives in a small but adequate apartment on the ground floor. A nearby grocery delivers her food. Neighbors are available when she needs assistance.

Protected

This environment has built-in protections so that the client has the necessary supports.

> A man, who is quite impaired, lives alone in a large old house which has been his home for many years. It can be reached only by a long flight of stairs. He cannot leave the house unaided.

Arrangements have been made for a part-time "home aide" who shops, prepares meals and does light housework. A volunteer takes him to church each week. A volunteer telephone service calls him every morning. On his doctor's orders, a visiting nurse gives him prescribed injections twice a week.

Potentially Unsafe

In this environment one or more basic social supports are lacking, unsatisfactory or in danger of being cut off; housing is deteriorating (hot water unavailable, heating inadequate, arrangement for garbage disposal lacking; safety and health hazards present, such as broken windows, shaky banister or unlighted staircase); the neighborhood is hazardous because of frequent muggings of older persons, prevalence of drunkenness or drug addiction, lack of access to needed facilities or transportation to reach them.

A couple, both in their late seventies, live in a public housing project in a rapidly changing and deteriorating section of town. The hilly terrain makes it difficult for them to get out to shop, do other errands or to visit friends. Their telephone was recently removed due to the change in state laws which denied public assistance payments for such purposes.

An elderly woman lives in her own home, without relatives or close friends. The heater is inadequate and she is unable to put on storm windows. She is unable to go up and down her front steps and has no one to help with shopping. She lives on canned food most of the time and cannot properly attend to affairs which require her to leave the house.

Dangerous or Critical

A social support is suddenly withdrawn through illness or death of a person who has been providing major care or a housing crisis endangering health and safety arises (utilities shut off due to nonpayment of bills, eviction notices given, dwelling declared unfit for human habitation).

A single woman, age seventy-six, lives alone in a large house in a low income area. The house is dilapidated; two small fires occurred due to bad wiring which was not properly repaired. For long periods, gas and water are shut off due to nonpayment of bills. She must get permission to carry water from other houses. The cluttered and dirty condition of her house, caused in large part by the presence of fourteen dogs which she shelters, has created strained relations with neighbors who are unsympathetic and not inclined to give help.

Classification of Clients

The following tables indicate the classifications of clients in all three cities at first contact and at the end of the first month.*

TABLE IX

FUNCTIONAL LEVEL OF CLIENT AT FIRST CONTACT
AND END OF FIRST MONTH

| | Houston | | | |
| | At First Contact | | End of First Month | |
Functional Level	No.	%	No.	%
Total	121	100.0	121	100.0
Self-determining	19	15.7	20	16.5
Marginally competent	38	31.4	39	32.2
Incompetent	34	28.1	35	28.9
Dangerously incompetent	30	24.8	27	22.3
	San Diego			
Total	118	100.0	118	100.0
Self-determining	37	31.6	33	28.0
Marginally competent	49	41.5	47	39.8
Incompetent	27	22.8	29	24.5
Dangerously incompetent	5	4.2	3	2.5
Not reported or indeterminate	0	0.0	6	5.0
	Philadelphia			
Total	91	100.0	*	*
Self-determining	9	9.9		
Marginally competent	48	52.7		
Incompetent	25	27.5		
Dangerously incompetent	2	2.2		
Indeterminate	7	7.7		

* Philadelphia reported the classification of clients only at the point of first contact.

It will be noted that of the total number of 330 clients classified as to functional capacity at first contact, 65 were rated as self-determining; 135 as marginally competent; 86 as incompetent; and 37 as dangerously incompetent. About two-thirds (221 cases) fell into the two middle categories of "marginally competent" and "incompetent." The same ratio generally holds in each of the three communities. It is at the extreme ends that

* See Appendix II for case histories with classifications indicated.

TABLE X

ENVIRONMENTAL SITUATION OF CLIENT AT FIRST CONTACT AND END OF FIRST MONTH

Environmental Situation	Houston			
	At First Contact		End of First Month	
	No.	%	No.	%
Total	121	100.0	121	100.0
Manageable (by client)	8	6.6	13	10.7
Protected	21	17.4	63	52.1
Potentially unsafe	48	39.7	38	31.4
Dangerous	44	36.4	6	5.0
Indeterminate	0	0.0	1	0.8
	San Diego			
Total	118	100.0	118	100.0
Manageable (by client)	35	29.7	32	27.1
Protected	29	24.6	31	26.3
Potentially unsafe	45	38.1	44	37.3
Dangerous	9	7.6	5	4.2
Not reported or indeterminate	0	0.0	6	5.1
	Philadelphia			
Total	91	100.0		
Manageable (by client)	19	20.9		
Protected	24	26.4		
Potentially unsafe	35	38.5		
Dangerous	6	6.6		
Indeterminate	7	7.7		

the community differences are apparent. About 25 percent of the cases in Houston are rated as "dangerously incompetent" as compared to 4 percent in San Diego and 2 percent in Philadelphia.

The same general situation holds in relation to environmental conditions. Out of the total of 330 clients, the environmental situations of 62 were rated as manageable at first contact; 74 as protected; 128 as potentially unsafe; and 59 as dangerous. Here again, the greatest community differences are at the extreme ends of the scale. A little over one-third of the environmental situations in Houston were rated as dangerous and a little over 6 percent, manageable. In the other two cities, environmental situations were rated as dangerous for roughly 7 percent and manageable for 20 to 30 percent. The number rated potentially unsafe is strikingly similar in all three cities, varying from 38.1 percent to 39.7 percent.

It is important to note the amount of movement from one category to another at the end of the first month. By and large, the ability to function showed no change that could be described as dramatic. The number of persons classified as dangerously incompetent was reduced by three persons in Houston, by two in San Diego. Environmental changes were more striking. At the end of the first month, the number of persons living in dangerous environmental situations in Houston was reduced from forty-four to six, and the number in a protected environment increased from twenty-one to sixty-three. In San Diego, the number of persons originally living in dangerous environment was reduced from nine to five.

The change in ratings which occurred at the end of the first month underscores the importance of prompt protective action when a dangerously incompetent person is also living in a dangerous environment. Often this means a change in the living situation since change in ability to function can only be improved over time. The nature and duration of services brought to bear on protective service problems will be discussed further in the following chapter.

Chapter V

The Protective Service Program

PLANNING SERVICE ON THE BASIS OF SPECIFIC NEED

In order to formulate an appropriate plan for service based on individual need and to provide some method of evaluating the effectiveness of the service program, analyses were made of the clients' needs and the services provided in relation to the functional and environmental classifications described in the previous chapter.

These analyses included identifying the type of primary service to be provided, the intensity of service likely to be needed and a more detailed study of the personal and environmental problems of each individual.

Evaluation checkpoints were set up at the end of the first and third months of service for clients receiving care on a short-term basis and at the end of nine months for clients needing long-term protective service.

Examples of this attempt to provide some order in the processes of diagnosis, provision of service and evaluation are described below.

Relation of Classification System to Nature and Intensity of Service

How the classification of the client by functional capacity and environmental situation relates to the primary plan of service is indicated by the following chart. Crosses are used to indicate more intensive service than usually required. Where no crosses occur, the service is presumed to be usual.

Functional Classification	Environmental Classification	Type of Primary Service	Intensity of Service
Self-determining	Manageable	Preventive	
Self-determining	Protected	Preventive	
Self-determining	Potentially unsafe	Supportive	
		Supportive	+
Self-determining	Dangerous	Supportive	++
Marginally competent	Manageable	Preventive-Supportive	
Marginally competent	Protected	Supportive	
Marginally competent	Potentially unsafe	Supportive	++
Marginally competent	Dangerous	Supportive-Surrogate	+++
Incompetent	Manageable	Supportive	+
Incompetent	Protected	Supportive	
Incompetent	Potentially unsafe	Supportive-Surrogate	++
Incompetent	Dangerous	Surrogate	+++
Dangerously incompetent	Manageable	(Does not apply)	
Dangerously incompetent	Protected	Supportive	++
Dangerously incompetent	Potentially Dangerous	Surrogate	+++
Dangerously incompetent	Dangerous	Surrogate	++++

Identifying Specific Needs

Having assessed the degree of functional capacity and adequacy of the environment, the protective service worker's next step was to determine each client's specific needs and to plan how they could be met. For purposes of analysis, eight potential areas of need for service were identified as follows:

1. *Incapacity in daily living.* (Need for help with personal care, to be provided by homemaker, home health aide, attendant or practical nurse.)
2. *Problem of physical health.* (Need for diagnosis and/or treatment to be provided by a physician, visiting nurse or treatment at a hospital or clinic.)
3. *Psychosocial problem.* (Need for counseling by social worker or treatment by a psychiatrist; in serious cases, provision of guardian or institutional care.)
4. *Inability to manage household.* (Need for homemaker, consistent help of a relative or friend.)
5. *Housing inadequacy.* (Need to change place of residence or to make current living environment manageable.)
6. *Economic inadequacy.* (Need to increase income by exploring eligibility for Old Age Assistance, Social

Security, employment or other sources of public and/or private funds.)

7. *Problems of financial management.* (Need for help in budgeting and paying of bills by protective service worker, friend or relative, or in serious cases by appointment of conservator.)

8. *Need for legal protection.* (Need for protection against personal or financial exploitation; for help in securing legacies or other entitlements through courts or securing court-appointed guardian, et cetera; to be provided by lawyer or judge with assistance of protective service worker and representatives of other professions if necessary.)

The severity of need was measured on a five-point scale ranging from "not a problem" to "full supervision needed."

At intervals beginning with the end of the first month, estimates were made of the extent to which the needs of each client had or had not been met. While it would not be anticipated that most needs could be satisfied in a short period of time, some progress could be measured since protective service clients are often referred at a time of crisis when some immediate action is required.

As the following table taken from special tabulations in Houston of 92 severely impaired persons indicates, the most frequent unmet need was for legal protection. The second most frequent unmet need was in the area of psychosocial problems. The relatively low percentage of unmet needs in housing and household management, particularly of the dangerously incompetent clients, reflects the fact that immediate change of environment (hospitalization or institutional care) had been required for many. The unmet needs of the marginally incompetent showed more uniform distribution among the eight areas of need.

These areas of need obviously have some overlap. Incapacity for daily living may or may not be the result of an undiagnosed and untreated illness; inadequate housing may or may not be the result of inadequate income.

TABLE XI

SEVERITY OF NEED

Area of Need (Only those classified in the two highest estimates of need are included.)	Numbers With Needs for Help Unmet* During First Month					
	Dangerously Incompetent (30 clients)		Incompetent (34 clients)		Marginally Incompetent (28 clients)	
	No.	%	No.	%	No.	%
Incapacity in daily living	5	16.7	6	17.5	5	17.8
Problem of physical health	6	20.0	4	11.8	6	21.4
Psychosocial problems	10	33.3	10	29.0	8	28.6
Inability to manage household	3	10.0	6	17.5	6	21.4
Housing inadequacy	3	10.0	7	20.6	5	17.8
Economic Inadequacy	6	20.0	7	20.6	6	21.4
Problems of financial management	6	20.0	8	23.3	6	21.4
Need for legal protection	22	73.3	15	44.0	4	13.4

* Some clients had unmet needs in more than one area. Hence, the total number of persons with unmet needs is greater than the number of clients. (Only those classified in the highest estimates of need are included.)

Nevertheless, this type of analysis served as a useful guide to staff in planning and in estimating the effectiveness of the program being carried out in meeting specific need. It also reflected the relationship of specific needs to functional capacity.

For example, in Houston, where a large number of clients were classified as "incompetent" or "dangerously incompetent," 69 percent of the clients were identified on initial contact as having serious needs in the psychosocial area. At the end of the first month, the prevalence of serious unmet needs in this area had been reduced to 34 percent. In relation to daily living, 63 percent were identified at the outset as needing "considerable" service or full supervision in the area of health. At the end of the first month, the percentage was reduced to 19.

In San Diego, where unsafe environments or inadequate living arrangements were major deficiencies, housing inadequacy was identified as being serious for 36 percent at intake. After a month, only 20 percent had "most or all needs unmet" in this area. Household management problems existed to a marked degree for 32 percent of the San Diego group. A month later, the percentage was reduced to 22 percent. These reductions were achieved in spite of the fact that they were made during the early learning period of providing protective service with an acute shortage of suitable housing for many of the elderly in the community and that homemaker service (a major resource for meeting household management problems) was arranged with considerable difficulty.

The unmet needs in situations which are often critical and require immediate action may indicate the lack of appropriate community resources. The large proportion of both dangerously incompetent and incompetent individuals needing legal protection in the preceding table is an accurate reflection of the difficulty in securing the help of a lawyer and the problem of obtaining guardians or conservators. It is interesting also to note the drop in the number of marginally competent persons needing legal protection, whose greatest unmet need is in the psychosocial area requiring counseling a social worker or psychiatrist.

Categories of Service

Change of Living Arrangements

In Houston, 27 percent of the protective service clients became permanently institutionalized. Another 48 percent made some change of residence, not necessarily permanent: 19 percent were hospitalized; another 19 percent entered nursing homes; 6 percent were admitted to a mental hospital; 4 percent were placed in foster homes following admission to a mental hospital. In assessing the reasonableness of this amount of environmental change, it should be noted that on admission to the service, 54 percent of Houston's protective service clients were bedridden, partially bedridden, confined to wheelchair, or housebound; that only 25 percent were living in "good" housing; that 24.8 percent were classified as dangerously incompetent; 36.4 percent as in a dangerous environmental situation; and another 39.7 percent in a potentially unsafe environmental situation.

By contrast, in San Diego where a much smaller number of those applying or referred were severely impaired or living in unsafe environments, only 3 percent of the clients had become institutionalized at the end of the first month and 19 percent had a change of residence. Five percent of San Diego's clients were hospitalized; 4 percent entered a nursing home; and 2 percent were admitted to a mental hospital. Six percent were placed in other types of facilities. By contrast also, on admission to the service, 26 percent of the San Diego clients were bedridden, partially bedridden, confined to wheelchair or housebound; 47 percent were living in "good" housing; 4 percent were classified as dangerously incompetent; 7.6 percent as in a dangerous environmental situation; and 38 percent in a potentially unsafe environmental situation.

Involuntary Intervention

Involuntary intervention in another person's affairs is distasteful to most persons. Professional social workers have been imbued with the doctrine that the function of a caseworker is to help a client reach his own decisions. Unquestionably, this doctrine of self-determination cannot be strictly observed in those protective service cases when the client is incompetent or severely impaired in functioning. The demonstrations in Houston and San Diego throw considerable light on the situations which require intervention as well as ways in which the decision was reached and the actions taken.

First, it must be recognized that the potential for intervention is the distinguishing characteristic of a protective service case. This fact was carefully interpreted to the communities in which the demonstrations took place. Most of the referrals came from responsible agencies or concerned individuals in the community. The sources ranking highest in the three communities were public welfare department, friend or neighbor, nurse in public or voluntary agency, relative, hospital or nursing home.* Other sources included clergy, the courts, landlord, physician in private practice, and police. It should be noted also that the nature of the problems which brought about the referral was serious and often critical.†

FREQUENCY AND NATURE OF INTERVENTION. Given these situations, it seems obvious that involuntary intervention would some-

---

* See Table VII, Sources of Referral.
† See Table VIII, Reasons for Referral.

times be inevitable if the client were to be protected. Records of action taken on behalf of, and without the consent of, the protective service clients were kept in Houston and San Diego. The records include the attempts to intervene and the outcome, as seen in the following table:

TABLE XII
INVOLUNTARY INTERVENTIONS

Type of Service	Houston			San Diego		
	Successful Outcome	Service Unavailable	Unable to Utilize	Successful Outcome	Service Unavailable	Unable to Utilize
Medical diagnosis	38	0	3	2	5	0
Medical treatment	29	10	5	2	4	0
Hospital physical care	16	1	2	1	4	0
Psychiatric diagnosis	15	2	6	1	4	0
Nursing home care	15	1	5	0	2	0
Financial assistance	15	4	4	4	3	0
Psychiatric treatment	13	2	5	1	2	0
Mental hospital care	10	1	1	0	2	0
Hospital psychiatric care	8	0	2	1	1	0
Guardianship	5	14	11	0	2	0
Fiscal agent (other than guardian or conservator)	2	3	0	1	0	0
Foster home care	0	0	2	0	2	0
Congregate care	0	0	2	0	2	0
Conservator	0	1	0	3	3	0
Total	166	40	48	16	36	0

A "successful outcome" means that the service sought was obtained. "Service unavailable" means that the specific service sought for a particular client could not be obtained for him at the time of intervention. "Unable to utilize" indicates that the service did exist in the community but lack of financial resources or some other reason prevented the protective service agency's securing the service. If the client refused the service, it could be imposed only by court order. If the client was unable or unwilling to accept or secure the services necessary for his own or the community's protection, judicial authority was used.

It will be noted that Houston had a substantially larger number of involuntary interventions than San Diego. Possible reasons for the difference are greater severity of the cases referred for protective service in Houston* and the difference in timing,

* See Table VIII.

since the Houston record was for the second year of service and the staff had developed more skill and support for involuntary intervention, while the San Diego record was for the first year of operation by a newly organized agency. It should be pointed out that the number of interventions had no relationship to the number of clients. In Houston, the one hundred sixty-six successful attempts to secure help through involuntary intervention were on behalf of fifty-one persons; in San Diego, sixteen such attempts were on behalf of seventeen persons.

Other points to be noted in the experience of the two programs are that in each community the largest number of involuntary interventions were for the purpose of securing a medical diagnosis and treatment.

Psychiatric diagnosis and financial assistance were high on both lists. Attempts to provide guardianship were relatively unsuccessful in both communities. In Houston's thirty attempts to secure guardianship, only five were successful. It proved impossible to secure a guardian in fourteen cases and impossible to utilize the service of a guardian in eleven, probably because of lack of funds. In the beginning, diagnostic or emergency medical treatment, especially in the home, was very difficult to secure. Eventually, the project staff were able to locate a few physicians who would make emergency home calls and so secured medical aid at home or at a medical facility for a large proportion of the cases in which intervention was attempted.

SANCTION AND COLLABORATION. The decision for involuntary intervention is not lightly made. It is, however, pertinent to note that there are a number of times (after hours or when consultation is not readily available) when the protective service social worker must intervene immediately. Except for emergencies when action was obviously required immediately without waiting for substantial help from others, decision was made by the agency with consultation among the staff and in many cases consultations were held with other agencies and/or concerned individuals. Though the agency itself provided the sole sanction for intervention, very substantial numbers of both professional and lay

persons were involved or "collaborated" in the decision to intervene as indicated in Table XIII. The list includes relative,
neighbor, friend, landlord, clergy, court's attorney, guardian,
police, physician, nurse, home aide, public welfare worker and
representatives of other social or health agencies. The types of
persons collaborating in making the decision are obviously similar
to those making referrals. Frequently, the same persons were
involved. It is noted that relatives were involved in a larger
percentage of referrals and interventions in Houston than in San
Diego. On the other hand, a higher proportion of "neighbors,
friends, landlords and clergy" were directly involved in San
Diego than in Houston.

TABLE XIII

COLLABORATORS IN INVOLUNTARY INTERVENTIONS

Type of Collaborator	Houston		San Diego	
	No.	%	No.	%
Total clients involved	51	100	17	100
Neighbor, friend, landlord, clergy	19	37.0	8	47.0
Relative	32	63.0	2	12.0
Courts	11	22.0	2	12.0
Attorney or guardian	5	10.0	3	18.0
Police or peace officers	8	16.0	2	12.0
Physician	27	53.0	5	29.0
Nurse or home aide	4	8.0	1	6.0
Public welfare worker	14	27.0	3	18.0
Other agencies—social worker or psychologist	1	2.0	3	18.0
Other	6	12.0	1	6.0

In Houston, family approval for involuntary intervention for
medical diagnosis was given in about two-fifths of the cases.
For medical treatment or mental hospital care, the proportion
of family approvals was somewhat less. In some situations,
approval of the family was supported by legal counsel.

Judicial approval was required for seven cases involving
"psychiatric treatment"; for nine involving "psychiatric diagnosis"; and for seven involving "medical treatment."

San Diego reported no situation requiring judicial approval
for intervention, though in two situations approval of both
relatives and legal counsel was obtained.

As noted previously, the comparison in numbers of involuntary interventions between the two communities is not statistically relevant since they are based on the second year of operation in Houston and the first year in San Diego. Other influencing factors are the difference in degree of impairment in the clients of the two programs.

Supportive Services

It is obvious that not all protective service clients require hospitalization, institutional care or change of residence. Nor do all clients require involuntary intervention or surrogate services. It was evident in the demonstrations that when appropriate supportive services and facilities were available, many elderly persons could remain safely in their own homes. Institutional care could be avoided, postponed or shortened. The major supportive services needed in the demonstrations were casework and counseling; medical diagnosis and treatment; a variety of visiting services to the home (visiting nurse, homemaker, home health aide, housekeeper, attendant or companion, someone to do heavy cleaning); and help with fiscal management.

Facilities most often needed were safe and appropriate housing for independent living; hospitals and clinics easily available; nursing homes; intermediate care facilities providing a range of personal and health services in which impaired elderly persons could maintain maximum capacity to function and at the same time secure the assistance they needed.

Often, of course, the supportive service needed by clients was help to secure added financial resources to enable them to take advantage of such services and facilities as were available in the community.

When supportive services and facilities are not available, there is no alternative to continued living in a protective institutional setting, whether or not it is geared to client's individual needs. Custodial care is often necessary because rehabilitative services are not available to help impaired persons regain or retain ability to perform the acts of daily living.

A more detailed account of how various kinds of services were actually used with individuals in the demonstration services will be found in the following section. It summarizes two analyses of services given to Houston and San Diego protective service clients on both short- and long-term basis and the relation of these services to their functional and environmental classifications.

LENGTH OF SERVICE

Contrary to the premise accepted by some practitioners* that protective service clients must be protected until death, the demonstration projects indicated that a majority of the cases were stabilized within a six-month period. In some cases, the service does continue until death—and after. These are usually those of lone persons without relatives or other persons to take responsibility. The protective service agency acts in lieu of family. The social worker is sometimes present at death and is often responsible for making funeral arrangements, disposing of assets and so forth.

However, most protective services are provided to meet an exigency. Some action must be taken in critical situations immediately or within a relatively short period if needless neglect, exploitation or crisis is to be avoided.

Some clues as to the length and nature of protective service resulted from two analyses of the demonstration records.

Analyses of Short-term Care

The first was a study of ninety-two severely impaired older persons in the Houston program. They were classified as dangerously incompetent, thirty; incompetent, thirty-four; and marginally competent, twenty-eight. All were in potentially unsafe or dangerous environmental classifications. Analysis of the services given immediately or during an initial three-month period are summarized here.

1. *Dangerously Incompetent (30 persons)*

SERVICES PROVIDED. This group, admitted to the program at or near crisis understandably received the greatest amount of institutional care. About two-thirds were removed from their homes by the end of the first month.

---

* See *Overcoming Barriers to Protective Services*, pp. 6-70.

During the first three months, eleven clients were institutionalized permanently. Two others were placed in foster home care permanently. Nearly four-fifths received some period of institutional care (hospital, mental hospital, nursing home, home for the aged).

Fourteen were in hospitals for periods ranging from two days to the full three months. Half of these were hospitalized for thirty-two days or longer.

Fifteen were in nursing homes for periods of fifteen days to three months. Ten of these were in a nursing home thirty-two days or longer. Seven required mental hospital care: two were hospitalized briefly for diagnosis; the others remained from fifteen days to two months.

All thirty clients in this category received casework service amounting to a total of three hundred and seventy-four hours. Amounts for each varied from one to fifty hours of service. The model group consisting of eight cases received from four to eight hours of casework service. Ten cases received thirteen or more hours. Casework time included work directly with the client and work with others on his behalf. Legal services were made available to five clients.

Diagnostic and/or medical treatment was provided to twenty-four patients. Nine were seen by psychiatrists. Visiting or public health nurse service ranging from one to forty-seven visits was arranged for seven. Only three were able to use home aide service because of the severity of mental disabilities. The number of visits of the aides ranged from seven to forty-seven.

CLASSIFICATION: ENVIRONMENTAL CHANGES AT END OF ONE MONTH: Major changes in the environmental situation were made during the first month, with improvement as shown in the following chart:

Environmental Situation	At First Contact	At End of One Month
Manageable by client	0	0
Protected	6	22
Potentially unsafe	4	4
Dangerous	20	4

FUNCTIONAL CLASSIFICATION CHANGES AT END OF THREE MONTHS. Of the original thirty clients in this category, at the end of three months, four were in an "inactive" status, with the protective service problem controlled (cases to be reopened if situation worsened); one had died; one could not be helped; one rejected the service; leaving twenty-three on active status. Four were reclassified as incompetent and one as marginally competent, leaving eighteen still classified as dangerously incompetent. Eight clients formerly classified as incompetent had regressed to the point of being reclassified as dangerously incompetent, making twenty-six clients in this classification at the end of the three-month period.

2. *Incompetent Clients (34 persons)*

These clients, classified as incompetent, while not in crisis, had serious physical and mental infirmities. Nearly 80 percent were judged to be unable to care for their health or their finances properly. Nearly two-thirds were confused and had difficulty in relating to other people. Some exhibited paranoid tendencies, were fearful and intermittently disoriented.

SERVICES PROVIDED. Services to the thirty-four clients classified as incompetent were similar but smaller in volume than those required by the dangerously incompetent. Twenty-seven were living in potentially unsafe or dangerous environments. One-third were removed permanently from their homes within the first month. Of the fifteen clients in dangerous environments, twelve were moved to safer living arrangements. Within the three-month period, seven were moved to nursing homes for extended or permanent care; three were hospitalized; two spent some time in psychiatric wards; two had moved in and out of nursing homes. Proportionately, hospital and nursing home care were considerably less than for the dangerously incompetent group, but the use of supportive services in the home increased.

All received casework assistance. Seven clients utilized case aides as well as case workers; four used home aides and four used nurses in the home.

Diagnostic and/or medical treatment was provided for about two-thirds of the clients. Psychiatric diagnosis was provided for four persons. Legal assistance was used for four.

ENVIRONMENTAL CLASSIFICATION CHANGE. Environmental problems were a particularly difficult factor in arranging protection for the functionally incompetent clients, with twenty-seven of the group of thirty-four living in potentially unsafe or dangerous situations. Changes to a protected environment for so many during the first month of service again illustrate successful intervention of the protective service agency as shown in the following chart.

Environmental Situation	*At First Contact*	*At End of Month*
Manageable by client	0	0
Protected	7	23
Potentially unsafe	12	8
Dangerous	15	3

FUNCTIONAL CLASSIFICATION CHANGES AT END OF THIRD MONTH. Of the original thirty-four clients classified as incompetent, nine were in inactive status with the protective problem stabilized through changes in environment or by other means; one had rejected the service; two had died, leaving twenty-two in active status. Eight were reclassified as dangerously incompetent, leaving fourteen of the original group. Four originally classified as dangerously incompetent and two as marginally incompetent were reclassified as incompetent, making the number in this classification twenty at the end of the three-month period.

3. *Marginally Competent Clients (28 persons)*

This group showed some psychic and behavioral disorders but they were less severe and more intermittent than in the other categories. For example, they were noted as having "poor judgment" in use of funds, in eating, in self-care and personal hygiene. A small number manifested unwarranted suspiciousness and generalized anxiety. Three were out of contact with reality part of the time and two sometimes wandered. However, they were able to function fairly well part of the time and generally to have less serious difficulties than those in the other two classifications.

SERVICES PROVIDED. The pattern of service provided reflect this marginal ability to function. Although inadequate housing was a major problem for this group, crisis situations which required an immediate move were less apt to arise. Eight moved during the first month into protected environments. Six went into institutions permanently and two moved into homes of relatives or friends. Others continued to live in unsound housing and a potentially unsafe environment. Some were helped to change certain environmental factors which gave added protection, though the housing itself remained undesirable. No changes in residence were made after the first month.

Twenty of the twenty-eight members of this group received casework service. Helping them often required greater amounts of time in the beginning since individuals with marginal competence often appear to be afraid of losing independence by admitting the need for assistance, and tend to resist service more than those with greater impairment. During the latter two months, the casework time was less, averaging seven and three-tenths hours per case (about half the time needed by the members of the other two categories). The "model" group received from one to four hours of casework. One client received twenty-five hours of service. There were no cases of involuntary intervention in this group, and none was seen by a psychiatrist. About half received diagnostic or treatment services by a physician.

Fewer were hospitalized and for shorter periods of time (three to seven days) than in the other categories. None required care in a mental hospital.

They also made less use of supportive services in the home. Four clients received visiting nurse service varying from two to eighteen visits. A home health aide was supplied to three clients, varying from two to sixty-two visits.

ENVIRONMENTAL CLASSIFICATION CHANGE. Twelve of the twenty-four clients whose environmental situation was considered "potentially unsafe" remained in that category. However, the social worker's ability to utilize the marginal ability of the client to function in changing the environmental situation is reflected in the following chart:

Environmental Situation	At First Contact	At End of One Month
Manageable by client	0	3
Protected	0	12
Potentially unsafe	24	12
Dangerous	4	1

FUNCTIONAL CLASSIFICATION CHANGES AT END OF THIRD MONTH. Of the original twenty-eight clients, three shifted to inactive status during the first month with the protective problem controlled; one rejected service; one moved out of the jurisdiction; two were the joint responsibility of other agencies; six were permanently institutionalized; two were reclassified as incompetent and one became dangerously incompetent. Two of the incompetent group had been classified as marginally competent. This left fourteen in this classification at the end of three months.

Analysis of Long-term Protective Services

The second analysis was made of protective services given to "long-term" clients in Houston and San Diego during the seventh, eighth and ninth months. At the end of six months after initial contact, twenty-six of the one hundred twenty-one cases in Houston (21.4 percent) and twenty-two of the one hundred eighteen cases in San Diego (18.5 percent) continued to receive services.

The classifications of this group are shown in the following table.

Functional Level and Environmental Situation—
Long-term Clients

TABLE XIV

PROBLEM/SITUATION OF LONG-TERM CLIENTS

Functional Classification	*Houston* No.	%	*San Diego* No.	%
Total	26	100.0	22	100.0
Self-determining	3	11.5	5	22.7
Marginally competent	11	42.3	9	40.9
Incompetent	6	23.1	8	36.4
Dangerously incompetent	6	23.1	0	0.0
Environmental Classification				
Manageable by client	2	7.7	6	27.0
Protected	13	50.0	10	45.5
Potentially unsafe	10	38.0	6	27.3
Dangerous	1	3.0	0	0.0

Nearly half of those in Houston and a little more than a third of those in San Diego who required long-term care were classified as incompetent or dangerously incompetent, indicating a need for continued surveillance.

It is evident that these clients had long-term problems with worsening situations which fluctuated in relation to critical health problems. For example, in Houston's dangerously incompetent classification at nine months, one of the clients was dying but being cared for by a spouse who needed casework support; another client was in the process of being committed to a mental hospital (this occurred in the tenth month) and four others were in protective care institutions, which had agreed to accept them only if casework support was continued.

Services Received

Many of the long-term clients were homebound. There were very few changes in residence; three in Houston and four in San Diego. Those who required a change were moved to a protective environment—to an institution or with friends or relatives. Some involuntary interventions were required during this period. Seven were reported in Houston and three in San Diego. In Houston, the action was taken by the agency with support of neighbors in two cases, with agreement of a relative in another case and with court action in the other four cases. In San Diego, a relative assisted with one and there was court action in one.

It is significant that these long-term cases had not required involuntary intervention until this period. Obviously, the situations had worsened to the point where the agency had no choice but to take action in behalf of the client.

In the Houston group, twenty-three received casework service averaging three and seven-tenths hours per case or eighty-five hours in all. No service was provided by case assistants. Volunteer "protectors" gave considerable help to clients, though no records of their service were kept. Ten clients received sixty-seven hours of casework service in San Diego. Casework assistants served sixteen clients, averaging sixteen and seven-tenths hours per case for a total of two hundred sixty-eight hours.

Services in the home varied widely for this group. Two cases in Houston received home aide service; one receiving thirty-five visits, the other ninety-five. One case in San Diego received eighteen visits. Three cases in Houston and two in San Diego had attendant service; four for one month and one for two months. One case in Houston and three cases in San Diego received nursing care in the home, varying from two to ten in the number of visits.

One case in Houston and three in San Diego were hospitalized for short periods of time. Three in Houston and two in San Diego received legal assistance. One in Houston and two in San Diego received psychiatric help.

At the end of nine months, financial management had been assumed by others for 50 percent of the Houston clients and 14 percent of those in San Diego. However, about a fourth of those "largely or totally unable to manage their affairs" had not received fiscal assistance because neither the agency nor the client had funds to pay for it, and no responsible relative or volunteer had been found.

Others were still in need of health service, personal care, legal protection and so forth, though these needs had been met for a substantial number.

Nine cases were closed during the three-month period. The service was no longer required to meet the needs of clients in two cases. Six were moved out of the area. One client died.

Both Houston and San Diego reported that a majority of their clients were willing to accept help from the protective service worker at the end of nine months; however, five of Houston's twenty-six clients and five of San Diego's twenty-two clients continued to deny the need for help or were reluctant to accept it. Four of the Houston cases and two in San Diego were unaware of any relationship to the worker.

SUMMARY

These two analyses confirm the differential approach needed in serving protective service clients. While the functioning capacity of the client in a particular environment plays a large role in the kind and intensity of services required to protect him, a definitive pattern of services does not emerge.

The analysis of short-term services with the severely impaired in dangerous or unsafe environments indicated immediate intervention which frequently required long-term hospitalization or permanent institutionalization and/or a variety of longer term service. By contrast, in most of the less critical cases: the marginally functioning in unsafe or dangerous environments, less drastic measures were required. But more time was needed to obtain their acceptance of environmental change and supportive services. Few of the marginally functioning clients required moving when they consented to service in their own homes.

In the analysis of longer term clients, involuntary intervention was not utilized because the majority were in protected or partially protected situations. Their fluctuating health problems in a variety of circumstances called for contacts by social workers and/or case aides. While numerous supportive services helped to protect these clients, it became evident that there continued to be outstanding unmet needs in health services, legal assistance, personal and home care. As the situations worsened, intervention became necessary for protection of some clients.

Chapter VI

Implications for Further Development of Protective Services

COMMUNITY NEED

THE RECORDING AND evaluation of experience of the three community demonstrations reveal certain common denominators of practice which help to advance the development of plans for protective service programs. These result from the successful accomplishment of protection of many older persons, as well as from the analysis of unresolved problems and inability to provide protection. Frequently, the lack of resources led to the frustration of workers, to delayed action which prolonged the suffering of elderly persons in need of help and sometimes to failure.

In all three communities, the need was underscored for a definite plan for protection for all impaired adults who cannot themselves secure the help they need. It became apparent as the demonstrations progressed that it was wasteful of human and community resources to allow the situations of these individuals to deteriorate to a point of crisis, when earlier intervention might prevent unnecessary suffering, long-term care or emergency interventions often requiring drastic action.

Continuation of the Demonstration Programs

One important evidence of community recognition of the necessity for protective service for older people is the fact that plans for continuing protective service programs were instituted in all three communities.

In Houston, the program has become a two-pronged service. Sheltering Arms, the original demonstration agency, has continued its counseling program for elderly persons, including some who require protective service. Serving the most severely impaired elderly persons is a new project funded by Title III of the Older Americans Act. Entitled, "Protective Mental Health Services for Adults," it is being conducted under the authority of the county judge. The project is part of the Mental Health Screening Service located in the Harris County Mental Health and Mental Retardation Center. The director of the screening service was the director of the Protective Service Demonstration Program of Sheltering Arms from 1966 to 1968. The new project staff is made up of three full-time specialists—a social worker, a public health nurse and a case aide—and three part-time specialists—a medical doctor, a psychiatrist and an attorney. The stated objectives of the new demonstration are "to build on the work already done in Houston (the work of Sheltering Arms and a study carried out by Baylor College of Medicine) and to provide maximum protection, restoration and maintenance of adults through a program operating from a legal-based agency. The project will provide surrogate services (as defined in the NCOA publication, *Overcoming Barriers to Protective Services for the Aging*) as the need for these services is brought to the attention of the county judge and his court."

In San Diego, the protective service program is being continued under the sponsorship of the County Mental Health Agency, established under the California Mental Health Act of 1968. The director of the NCOA demonstration was appointed as director of the new program in San Diego. Both the Houston and San Diego programs will serve adults of any age who need protective service, including the retarded, mentally ill or others severely disabled.

In Philadelphia, the program was strengthened and extended under the continuing auspice of the City's Department of Public Welfare, Adult Services Division, with the same director. There has been an increase in the number of professional staff and the number of homemakers, together with higher salary scales which have resulted in more stable staff and improved services. Foster home care (as well as counseling and institutional placement) have been extended. One particularly worrisome problem to the director—that of emergency shelter—has been worked out through the combined efforts of the protective service program, the police department, public and private hospitals, and the county home. The police directive that has instructed placement of the homeless in the county home or county jail has been revoked. Instead, the Standby Casework Personnel of the Adult Department are immediately involved in an Emergency Medical and Social Diagnostic Service on a twenty-four hour basis. The protective service social worker coordinates the services of the hospitals in providing emergency physical examinations and the county home in giving temporary shelter so that persons found wandering in the streets are no longer put in jail.

Community Responsibility for a Protective Service System

The term, "community responsibility," is often used to dilute the sense of personal obligation to the point that nobody feels it is his duty to assume leadership. The responsibility for seeing that some resource for protection is available to infirm adults seems clearly to fall on that group of individuals who in one way or another have assumed or accepted or been elected to some position of leadership in relation to health and welfare services. The group may include public officials; professional personnel who are executives or practitioners in public or voluntary social and health agencies; or volunteers who serve as board members or in other leadership positions. Responsibility for specific action may be assigned to one or more agencies but it must be clear that any such agency must have the active support and cooperation of all pertinent community resources.

If the community is to be well served, its leaders in health and welfare will need to take cognizance of new and innovative developments in provision and delivery of services and to seek out all available sources for funding, both private and governmental. Some community funds, foundations and other resources for private funding have contributed substantially to programs in the field of aging. Others are in the process of re-ordering their priorities in giving in view of emerging new needs. For a number of years, it has been possible to provide services to older people through public welfare agencies on a liberal matching grant formula. Such services, which include protective services and homemaker services, must be part of the state welfare "plan" to secure the federal funds. Many states have not taken advantage of this opportunity. Many communities were not aware of the possibility or the fact that these services would eventually be mandatory. Other federal agencies have funded programs which have relevance for protective services. These include legal services for the poor under the Office of Economic Opportunity; improved delivery systems of surplus foods and provision of food stamps under the Department of Agriculture; rent supplements and low interest long-term loans to voluntary agencies for construction of rental housing for low-income elderly under the Department of Housing and Urban Development; and numerous other government programs which can help fund or provide facilities and services with a minimum of expenditure of local funds. There have also been grants for a wide variety of research and demonstration programs and for training through the Older Americans Act, either directly from the Administration on Aging in the Department of Health, Education and Welfare or from the State Offices on Aging established under the Act.

Grants under the Older Americans Act, as well as numerous other government resources, have been for limited time only, usually three years. It is often necessary and wise to secure funds on a limited term demonstration basis to get a program started and to test its validity. This action should be taken, however, in full realization that the need for the service is not of limited duration and that the demonstration period must be seen as providing the opportunity to explore community needs and resources and to work out some feasible way to incorporate the service program into the health and welfare service system.

The Lake case referred to in the opening chapter of this report set a legal precedent for community responsibility to provide alternatives to care in a mental hospital for persons who neither require nor benefit from such an institution. The legal requirement does not apply outside the District of Columbia. The responsibility, however, applies nationwide.

THE PROTECTIVE SERVICE AGENCY

The three demonstrations illustrated that no single type of agency sponsorship is essential to a protective service program. A public agency, a voluntary agency which extended its program to include protective service and a new agency organized for the sole purpose of giving protective service—all had obvious advantages and drawbacks. Changes in sponsorship at the end of the demonstration programs showed new possibilities. While there appears to be general agreement that the core professional responsibility should be carried by a social worker, it does not follow that the program must necessarily be in a social agency. Social workers can be and are employed by many other agencies and organizations. Theoretically, a case can be made for sponsorship of protective service by a health agency since physical and mental health programs are crucial factors in nearly all protective service cases.*

The relationship between the County Court and the County Mental Health Center in Houston also presents significant opportunities for innovative collaboration.†

There may be a question of preference as to public versus voluntary auspice. Public welfare departments as sponsors of protective service programs appear to have three obvious advantages and two handicaps. They exist in all communities; they have the possibility of a generous formula of matching federal funds; and they can provide or purchase such services as homemaker or guardianship. The handicaps are that in many states public welfare services are traditionally limited to persons receiving Old Age Assistance and that some persons reject a public welfare service as carrying a stigma. It should be noted, however, that there is a federal mandate separating money payments and service in public welfare. This permits public welfare departments to provide services to persons who are "potential" but not

---

* In Cleveland, Ohio, after the completion of a protective service research project sponsored by a voluntary social agency with federal funding, an on-going protective service program was established in a community health agency in 1969.

† Though the cases are not parallel, it may be interesting to note that in New York City, responsibility for children in need of protection has been transferred from the Family Court to the Department of Social Services.

current recipients of Old Age Assistance. These changes in administration may make public welfare services more acceptable to many older persons in need of protective service and to those concerned with securing resources for their protection.

It will be important for all persons concerned with protection of elderly persons to keep in close touch with developments in their state and local departments of public welfare.

On the other hand, under current conditions and in some communities, a voluntary agency, if adequately funded, may find it easier to work with all segments of the elderly population and to move with greater ease among the multiplicity of public and voluntary agencies and individuals involved in protective service programs. Also, some groups and individuals may be more comfortable in referring relatives, friends or clients to a voluntary rather than to a public agency.

At present, there are relatively few agencies which serve "all adults in need of protection." As experience grows under the federal mandate to states for the organization of protective services for adults, it may be feasible for public welfare departments to provide the leadership in mobilizing community resources for a protective service system. This could combine funding from public as well as voluntary sources. Since no one agency has all of the services required of such a system, the public welfare department might provide the coordinating social work services and/or other supporting services or obtain them through contracts with voluntary agencies. In local communities where voluntary agencies have established protective services which have the support of the community, it may also be more feasible for public welfare to contract for the coordinating social work. This process would permit greater flexibility in serving all adults in need of protection, regardless of income.

Whatever the auspice, it seems clear from analysis of procedures in the demonstration programs that certain qualities are essential to any agency providing protective service. They include (a) commitment to carrying out a difficult task of resolving differential problems of adults who need protection; (b) willingness to accept the risks and responsibilities of involuntary intervention; (c) leadership in securing the community resources necessary to performing a protective service function; (d) an established reputation for high standards of service which will command the respect of community agencies and professional leaders; and (e) a protective service program for elderly persons which is a collaborative community venture in which many agencies and individuals play a part.

PROTECTIVE SERVICE STAFF

Core Leadership

The experience of the three NCOA demonstrations and of other experimental programs around the country seems to support the opinion that social work can serve as the core profession in a protective service program, with a social worker as its director. It was usually the social worker who provided the initiative and coordination of services which results in avoidance or reduction of crisis. The professional education of a social worker is designed to equip him with the specific social and psychological skills to deal with persons under stress, particularly when primary needs are understanding of the environment of the impaired older person, techniques of community organization, ability to work effectively with many types of persons (professional and nonprofessional), and knowledge of community resources, all of which are essential skills of the protective service worker.

The social worker's basic practice of helping individuals to make independent judgments about managing their lives and mobilizing their own strengths for appropriate action must be modified in dealing with persons whose disabilities render them incapable of making the right decisions or of taking action which serves their own best interests. The willingness to take action in emergencies, to exercise involuntary intervention when necessary to protect the client's well-being and to defend this professional judgment appear to be the distinguishing marks of a professional protective service worker which earn him the respect and cooperation of other professional persons. In assuming the surrogate role, the social worker must have a clear understanding of the law as it relates to the situation and a close professional relationship with a legal consultant concerned and knowledgeable about protective problems together with complete support of the agency which he is functioning in this role. Development of the skill of intervention before crisis is based on social work skills, knowledge of the law, and above all, experience in dealing with protectice service clients.

The senior case worker in the San Diego project wrote as follows about the development of this skill during the first year of the project:

> In the area of client relationships, as well as in the application of legal authority, we did have our rather serious hangups; but we managed to live with them and to examine and re-examine our procedures in order to be as sure as possible that we were doing our clients more good than harm. . . . Serious errors were considered unlikely if each worker acted from his knowledge, his conscience, and the best interests of the client.

The director of the Houston program emphasized courage as the primary personal qualification for a protective service worker. At the end of the first year of the demonstration, she described it as follows:

> Courage, means the courage of your own convictions, and the courage to consider new and unorthodox methods of solving problems. It takes courage to be cross-examined in court and defend your professional opinion about a situation. It takes courage to oppose a relative who is exploiting a client and to intervene in this family relationship. It takes courage to confront a confused and hostile aged person with the realities of his situation. It takes courage to trust your own judgment and perhaps leave a client in a precarious situation because you are convinced that the danger to his life is not as great as the danger to his self-respect. Most of all, it takes a lot of courage to confront a complicated situation where there is community 'uproar,' and retain your independent judgment about the welfare of the client.

Professional Collaboration

Through the experience already gained, it is clear that if a protective service program is to work effectively, at least four professional groups must be involved. They are social work, physical medicine, psychiatry and law. Collaborative effort among these groups may be extremely difficult to achieve. Social workers may need to win acceptance as equals among other professional practitioners. In some communities, such acceptance is still rare. That this situation is due largely to lack of experience in professional collaboration was borne out by the demonstrations. There were evidences in the reports of frustrating and even agonizing attempts to secure the medical, psychiatric or legal help needed. Payment for professional services often presented difficulties. Current patterns of practice among most professional groups are not geared to the need of elderly, impaired or even indigent individuals. Physicians are increasingly unaccustomed to making home calls. Psychiatrists seldom do. Thus, they are understandably loathe to visit a patient who rejects treatment, though he may be desperately in need of it. Hospitalization or other remedial action is often impossible without a doctor's order and a doctor is not likely to issue such orders for a patient he has not seen. Since it was often virtually impossible to transport protective service clients to a doctor, the social workers found it essential to develop a relationship with at least one physician who would trust their judgment and could be counted on to come to the aid of a client when requested to do so. Even so, the experience of patients shunted from one type of treatment facility to another is one of the least pleasant aspects of a number of case histories.

It has been pointed out that from the legal point of view, much remains to be done in harmonizing the requirements of law with new social, medical and psychiatric concepts, particularly in eliminating the vestiges of criminal law and procedure in providing protective service for the mentally disabled. The services of a qualified attorney, interested in and knowledgeable about mental impairment of aged persons, were even more difficult to secure than those of a doctor. Since none of the projects had funds to employ legal counsel and most of the clients were too poor to pay lawyer's fees, the workers for the most part relied on legal advice from interested lawyers on a volunteer basis. This method often did not provide sufficient time for legal consultation when it was needed. Many attorneys were not well enough acquainted with the legal problems of older people to be of much help. Some, however, became increasingly interested and helpful as they learned on a case-by-case basis how to deal with legal aspects of difficult individual problems. Progress in appropriate intervention is not possible without at least one attorney who can be counted on to assess the legal aspects of the protective service problem.

In Philadelphia, the legal services of the city solicitor were available. This arrangement was not wholly without problems since the city solicitor's general responsibilities as advocate for the city did not prepare him to understand the problems of the protective service client. In both Houston and San Diego, relationships with members of the medical and legal professions were worked out on a case-by-case basis, enlisting the interest of concerned individuals.

Under the leadership of skilled social workers and for the duration of a limited term demonstration, these efforts were, on the whole, remarkably successful. Under the circumstances, this person-to-person method was undoubtedly the only one open to the project workers, since it was often necessary to convince members of the medical and legal professions that it was possible to protect and often rehabilitate severely impaired elderly persons. But for the long run, such a method is unsound for itself or its further development and places an unjustified burden on the social worker as well as the members of the legal and medical professions.

Relationships between the protective service agency and these professional practitioners, who are essentially entrepreneurs, need to be in some sense "institutionalized." The success of one of the first protective service programs for elderly persons may be in large part attributed to the fact that the sponsoring Family Service Agency in Chicago, after consultation with the Community Service Society of New York, had an established working relationship with the Legal Aid Society. The protective service agency needs to establish appropriate relationships with representatives of the essential collaborative professions as part of the planning and organization process. This can be done in a number of ways. They can be employed as consultant's or part-time staff. Their services may be secured through arrangements on a fee or volunteer basis with firms, agencies or individuals. Whatever the arrangement, the ongoing interest, professional skill and reasonable allotment of time of a nucleus of representatives of the essential professions must be assured before a program of protective service can be undertaken.

A great need of the professional community is to accept the principle of collaborative effort among practitioners as equals with a rotating leadership dependence on current status or need of it. A protective service program offers an unusual opportunity for experimentation in ways of working out the most effective methods of collaboration in practice.

Paraprofessional Staff

Aides and/or neighborhood volunteers are essential adjuncts to any protective service program. The use of case aides in social work is a developing practice, which has proved particularly successful in outreach programs for older persons.

The San Diego program in particular made use of nonprofessional personnel to perform a multitude of time-consuming tasks which did not require the services of a trained social worker. At some points, the aide (often belonging to the same racial, ethnic and social group as the client) was better able than the professional staff to establish a relationship and effectively influence a resistive client to accept a plan of action crucial to his well-being. Philadelphia employed homemakers as a regular part of the agency staff and used them in somewhat similar ways in the protective service program.

Lacking case aides as part of the basic staff, Houston made impressive use of neighbors as volunteers. Agencies will need to take into account the professional time required to recruit and maintain some oversight of these neighbor volunteers. The personal value to an elderly person of the interest and help of a neighbor cannot be ignored. (It was pointed out that these neighbors who were readily available on an "as needed" basis performed quite a different function from that of volunteers supplied through a volunteer bureau of members of a formally organized "friendly visitor" program.)

It would seem wise to include aides on the staff to insure continuity of nonprofessional or paraprofessional assistance to the clients, to employ homemakers when needed and to add as much volunteer service on a personal, neighborly basis as possible.

COMMUNITY RESOURCES

Aside from his personal and professional skills, the protective service worker needs certain essential tools. He must have available a minimum number of facilities and services. The county or city home and the state hospital are no longer acceptable as the only repositories of the community's mentally and physically frail elderly. Different kinds of institutional care facilities for the elderly have demonstrated the values of a variety of facilities to meet graduations of need, such as those providing skilled nursing care; those which provide private rooms, a central dining room and some personal care when needed; and the foster home which offers family environment.

It was clear from these demonstrations as well as research carried out by hospitals and other community agencies that many elderly persons live out their lives in institutions because they have no home or other place to go, or there is no other way to secure help with certain personal or household tasks.

If unnecessary institutional care is to be avoided, elderly impaired persons must have, as a minimum, safe and convenient housing at incomes consistent with their rent. Many will need alternate resources for institutional services available to them in their own homes. Among these are home-delivered meals and the service of a visiting nurse, home health aide, therapist, homemaker, household aide, "friendly visitor" or someone to make a "reassurance" telephone call regularly. The need for occasional "heavy cleaning" was evident in the demonstrations. For lack of availability of such help, social workers and aides undertook unbelievable tasks of removing accumulated filth and junk from the houses and yards of clients.

In many communities, new agencies have been created or

established agencies have modified their traditional practices to provide some of these social tools. One of the most urgently needed resources for giving adequate protection is that of persons capable and willing to serve as guardians or fiscal agents for elderly persons with small incomes and little or no property. Except in a few states which provide such service for Old Age Assistance recipients, such a resource is generally unavailable. Much experimentation remains to be done in this area of need.

A final need of the protective service program is a well-publicized information and referral service with follow-up of referral where elderly persons or their relatives and friends can get assistance in obtaining whatever services—preventive, supportive or surrogate—the community provides.

SUMMARY: NEW DIRECTIONS

The demonstration programs have recorded a substantial body of information which can assist communities throughout the country. However, these and other experimental programs of protective service have not refined the process of giving protection to elderly persons to the point of justifying a set of guidelines and situations applicable to all communities.

All practice seems to indicate that the resolution of the complicated problems found in adult protection can never be reduced to a simple formula. The serious and diverse nature of the medical, psychological, social and/or legal problems leaves no choice but to proceed with the differential case-by-case approach.

Numerous unanswered questions concerning the components of protective services remain to be explored, tested and evaluated. Two of the most urgent unsolved problems are (a) adequate coordination and continuity of services and (b) securing appropriate legal protection through statutory changes where needed and, as indicated previously, provision for employment and supervision of guardians, conservators or other fiscal agents for persons with limited financial resources who need such help.

Additional experience in dealing with these and other administrative and service problems is needed before the most effective methods of safeguarding impaired elderly persons from the "harm of neglect and exploitation" can be set forth in detail.

Nevertheless, substantial progress has been made in understanding the nature of the need for protection of older adults and the techniques by which protection can be given without disregarding the rights of the individual to self-determination to the fullest extent of his capability.

The demonstrations (described here and the experience gained from other programs in protective service) indicate these new directions.

Broadening the Identification of the Client

The client has become identified as the impaired elderly adult who is unable to obtain the help he needs to sustain his own well-being, and who is without others able and willing to assume this responsibility. Though the majority of the protective service clients in the demonstrations were over seventy-five years of age, the program should be prepared to serve incapacitated adults of all ages who need protection.

Auspices and Characteristics of Protective Service Agencies

A protective service program for adults can be administered by various types of agencies, public or voluntary, with the following characteristics and resources:

- Commitment to protect incapacitated adults and aid them to live at their maximum level of functioning in safety and comfort.
- Access to the essential professional services of social work, law, medicine and psychiatry, and public health, with consideration of environmental problems.
- Willingness to modify traditional methods of practice in all professional disciplines which may impede the prompt delivery of protective services.
- Protective service staff workers who have the attitudes, skills, courage, resourcefulness and other personal characteristics which enable them to relate effectively to impaired (often rejecting) clients and to work expeditiously with

all other professionals and nonprofessionals who can be of assistance to the client.

• Availability of supportive services which should include the following: information and referral service; housekeeper, homemaker and home health aides, medical assistance including physician's services (home calls in emergencies), hospitals, convalescent and nursing homes, rehabilitation services, visiting nurses, psychiatric, diagnostic and treatment services; housing which insures safety and well-being; adequate public assistance programs; appropriate resources for diagnosis and care in emergency situations; public health services to remedy environmental situations harmful to individuals and the community or neighborhood.

The Delivery System: A Comprehensive Approach

Protective services call for a comprehensive approach, which includes preventive, supportive and surrogate services. Agency operation requires willingness to learn how to provide promptly protective measures which safeguard the individuals' well-being, comfort and safety and to "do or get others to do whatever is necessary to meet the demands of the situation."*

The comprehensive approach implies:

• New methods of community interpretation and case finding.
• An outreach program to locate the hard-to-reach isolated adults.
• Initiating methods of prompt intervention appropriate to individual need.
• Instituting available service promptly to meet emergencies of new or former clients.
• Taking leadership in developing interdisciplinary collaboration.

----

* Blenkner, Margaret; Wasser, Edna, and Bloom, Martin: *Protective Services for Older People: Progress Report for 1966-67.* Cleveland, Benjamin Rose Institute, 1967. p. 77.

- Serving as the catalyst to mobilize and engage community resources.
- Organizing the training of nonprofessionals and volunteers.

The Surrogate Function

The principle of *parens patria* operates when the exigencies of the situation require action to protect the client. Sanction and support for acting in behalf of another result from the following:

- A clear understanding of the law and its administrative procedures in relation to the protective service client.
- Constructive working relationships with the probate court and a legal consultant who is actively working with protective services.
- Access to diagnostic assistance from the medical, legal and psychiatric consultants who are specialists in working with impaired adults or who are willing to learn ways in which intervention can be accomplished in the best interests of individuals to preserve their rights and well-being.
- Demonstration of professional responsibility and diagnostic acuity of the protective service staff.
- Active participation of a technical advisory committee, composed of legal, medical, psychiatric and financial experts from both public and voluntary sectors who have continuing concern for finding solutions to the presently unresolved protective problems.

The demonstrations described in this report have added substantially to the knowledge about providing protective service to the elderly. They show that such a service is needed in every community. They show with equal clarity that the emphasis is on protecting and serving the client rather than on any particular type of agency or on specified program content. Protective service requires a personal plan to meet individual needs. As preventive and supportive services are developed, as environmental conditions improve, the incidence of crisis situations needing the surrogate aspects of protective care will hopefullly decrease. It may even be that eventually the essentials of protective service will be recognized as essentials of the social structure of the community, utilizing the combined resources which exist and creating those that are needed but do not exist. Even now, communities do not need special agency structure so much as a genuine commitment to use and develop further whatever resources they have or can secure to help older persons in need of protection obtain services appropriate to their safety and comfort.

APPENDICES

Appendix I

Selected Bibliography

Alexander, George J.: Surrogate Management of the Property of the Aged. *Syracuse Law Review*, XXI, Fall, 1969.

Allen, Richard C.: *Mental Impairment and Legal Incompetency.* New York, Prentice-Hall, 1968, p. 401.

Blenkner, Margaret; Wasser, Edna, and Bloom, Martin: *Protective Services for Older People: Progress Report for 1966-67.* Cleveland, Benjamin Rose Institute, 1967, p. 77.

Blenkner, Margaret: Service and Survival. Paper presented at the 8th International Congress of Gerontology, Washington, D.C., August 26, 1969. Cleveland, Benjamin Rose Institute, 1969, p. 15 (Mimeographed).

Booth, F. Estelle: *Reaching Out to the Hard to Reach Older Person.* San Francisco, San Francisco Senior Center, 1969, p. 40.

California: *Mental Health Act. Welfare and Institutions Code.* (1969).

Follett, Sally: Protective Services Through the Auspices of a Public Welfare Department. Paper presented at the National Conference on Social Welfare, San Francisco, May 1968. San Jose (Calif.), Santa Clara Public Welfare Department, p. 9 (Mimeographed).

Fraser, George B.: Guardianship of the Person. *45 Iowa Law Review,* p. 231. (1960).

Garrettson, Jane: Protective Services for Older People. Implications for Public and Voluntary Agencies. Paper presented at the National Conference on Social Welfare, 1968. Chicago, Family Service Bureau, United Charities (Mimeographed).

Hall, Gertrude H.: Protective Services for Adults. *Encyclopedia of Social Work,* 16th Issue. New York, National Association of Social Workers, 1971, p. 999-1007.

Hall, Nancy M.: *Project of Special Services to the Aging.* Winston-Salem, Forsyth County Public Welfare Department, 1965, p. 31.

Kalish, Richard A. (Ed.): *The Dependencies of Old People.* Occasional Papers on Gerontology, No. 6. Ann Arbor, Institute of Gerontology, University of Michigan, Wayne State University, 1969, p. 106.

Lehmann, Virginia, and Mathiasen, Geneva: *Guardianship and Protective Services for Older People.* Washington, D.C., National Council on the Aging, 1963, p. 184.

Lowenthal, M.; Beckman, P., *et al.*: *Aging and Mental Disorder in San Francisco.* San Francisco, Jossey Bass, 1967.

Martin, John B.: Protective Services for the Aging. Paper presented at the Protective Services Workshop, San Diego, April 1970. Washington, D.C., Administration on Aging, U.S. Department of Health, Education and Welfare, p. 13 (Mimeographed).

McKeany, Maurine, and Taylor, Hazeltine Byrd: Public Guardians and Welfare Services in California. Final report of a research project supported by the Social and Rehabilitation Service, U.S. Department of Health, Education, and Welfare (CRD 365), School of Social Welfare, University of California, Berkeley, November 1970, p. 747.

McRoberts, Agnes: Protective Services for Adults: Issues and Principles for Social Casework. Houston, Sheltering Arms, 1967, p. 20 (Mimeographed).

McRoberts, Agnes: Protective Services Through the Auspices of a Voluntary Casework Agency. Paper presented at the National Conference on Social Welfare, San Francisco, May 1968. Houston, Sheltering Arms, p. 6 (Mimeographed).

Misbach, Henrietta: *Some Ethical and Procedural Problems in Providing Protective Services*: *Protective Services, San Diego.* San Diego, Adult Protective Services, 1970, p. 9 (Mimeographed).

Morris, Robert: Aging and Field of Social Work. In *Aging and the Practicing Professions.* Vol. II: *Aging and Society,* edited by M. W. Riley. New York, Russell Sage Foundation, 1969.

National Conference of Commissioners on Uniform State Laws: *Uniform Probate Code.* St. Paul (Minn.), West Publishing Company, 1970.

National Conference of Lawyers and Social Workers: Adult Protective Services: Responsibilities and Reciprocal Relationships of the Lawyer and Social Worker. Publication No. 5. New York, National Association of Social Workers, October 1967, p. 9.

National Council on the Aging: *A Crucial Issue in Social Work Practice*: *Protective Services for Older People.* Proceedings of two sessions of the National Conference on Social Welfare. Washington, D.C., 1966, p. 55.

NCOA: *Overcoming Barriers to Protective Services for the Aged.* Report of a National Institute on Protective Services, Houston, Texas, January 1968. Washington, D.C., National Council on the Aging, 1968, p. 129.

NCOA: *The Golden Years . . . A Tarnished Myth.* Washington, D.C., The National Council on the Aging, January 1970.

NCOA: *The Law and the Impaired Older Person: Protection or Punishment?* Proceedings of a session of the 15th Annual Meeting of the National Council on the Aging. Washington, D.C., 1966, p. 51.

Pennsylvania Citizens Council's Commission on Aging: *Pennsylvania Conference on Protective Services for Older People.* Harrisburg, State Department on Aging, 1965.

Pennsylvania Department of Public Welfare: Protective Services for Older People. 30-minute sound film. Harrisburg, State Commission on Aging, 1967.

Toward a Public Policy on Mental Health Care of the Elderly. Report No. 70, Vol. VII. New York, Committee on Aging of the Group for Advancement of Psychiatry, November 1970.

Twente, Esther: *Never too Old.* San Francisco, Jossey Bass, 1971.

United Cerebral Palsy Association: *Conference on Protective Services for the Handicapped.* Proceedings. November 15-17, 1966. New York, United Cerebral Palsy Association, p. 98.

U.S. President's Council on Aging: *Federal Payments to Older Persons in Need of Protection.* Report of a survey and conference. Washington, D.C., U.S. Government Printing Office, 1965, p. 66.

U.S. President's Task Force on Aging: *Toward a Brighter Future for the Elderly.* Report. Washington, D.C., 1970, p. 60.

U.S. Social and Rehabilitation Service: Report of the National Protective Service Project for Older Adults. Washington, D.C., U.S. Dept. Health, Education and Welfare, 1971 (153 pp.–$1.25).
The reports of two demonstration projects and guidelines for state and local governments for initiation of protective services for older adults.

U.S. Veterans Administration: Protective Services for the Aging. Tenth Annual Workshop. Fayetteville (Arkansas), Fayetteville Veterans Administration Hospital, 1966, p. 50.

U.S. Veterans Administration: Protective Services for the Aging. Third Annual Social Work Service Institute. Miami Veterans Administration Hospital, 1968. p. 102.

Wasser, Edna: *Creative Approaches in Casework with the Aging.* New York, Family Service Association of America, 1966, p. 98.

Case Histories

Case I. Mr. Austin: Middle-Age Breakdown—
Rehabilitation in Old Age

M R. AUSTIN, A seventy-eight-year-old white man, in his youth had been a minor league baseball player whose success at bat earned him the nickname, "Hitter." Later, he became a successful plumber, married and became the father of two children. During his middle fifties, heavy drinking culminated in chronic alcoholism, and he deserted his wife and family. When he was divorced, he gave his wife all the community property.

Living in flophouses, he developed tuberculosis which resulted in a two-year hospitalization. When he recovered, heavy drinking continued to be a problem. He worked at intermittent jobs until he was sixty-five, when he retired on Social Security and Old Age Assistance.

At this time, he became so hostile that it was necessary for the Department of Public Welfare to assign a male welfare worker to his case. A circulatory disorder resulted in gangrene and the removal of one leg. After three weeks in a convalescent hospital, he returned to his room in the slums. He became so alienated from the people in his neighborhood that he went three blocks by wheelchair to get his own groceries.

Despite his circulatory disorder, he refused medical care. Finally, when his other leg became affected, a visiting nurse was called in. Since he was unwilling to go to the hospital, home health aides were utilized to try to assist him with his daily living. He was incontinent and living in filth. His room was infested with roaches, mice and rats. He was determined not to accept help and threatend to shoot the home health aide if she were to return. At that time, the Visiting Nurse Association withdrew their service and referred the case to the protective service agency.

The protective service worker found Mr. Austin with a high temperature and in great pain. Despite strong objections, he was persuaded to go by ambulance to the hospital. For three days, his condition was critical.

The protective service worker located his daughter, who had had no contact with her father in twenty years. She at first refused to take any responsibility for him because of her childhood memories of his antisocial behavior. Her husband, however, seemed genuinely interested and concerned. Finally, the daughter agreed to sign a release for surgery. Her husband closed his father-in-law's room and stored his possessions.

Mr. Austin made a remarkable recovery from surgery. As he began to feel better physically, his attitude toward the doctors and the protective service worker began to improve. Initially, he had been resistant and hostile to any suggestions. The protective service worker helped build his self-esteem by visiting him regularly and showing concern for his physical comfort, obtaining a radio and insisting that he have new pajamas and robe. His appearance began to change.

The social worker also persuaded the daughter to assume responsibility for her father's checks and encouraged her to shop for certain articles which he needed. Thus, the daughter began to see more and more of her father. Eventually, the grandchildren were brought to visit their "Grandpa." One of the grandsons, very much interested in baseball, became fascinated by his grandfather's experience in minor league baseball.

After three months of protective care which included hospital care, physiotherapy and family interest, Mr. Austin was able to go to a nursing home located in the daughter's neighborhood. In the meanwhile, capitalizing on a dormant interest, the worker had encouraged him to do leather craft. Tools and supplies were obtained, and it soon became obvious that he had talent and ability. He received three months' worth of orders through a senior center gift shop.

By this time, Mr. Austin had been transformed from a hostile, severely handicapped and ill, dangerously incompetent, angry man to a pleasant, distinguished looking grandfather with a concerned family, new interests and a profitable craft.

Initial Classifications: Functional: incompetent. Environmental: dangerous.

Final Classifications: Functional: self-determining. Environmental: protected.

Case II. Mrs. Bell: Alone and Helpless

Mrs. Bell, an eighty-two-year-old Negro woman, was found by the police locked in her house and unconscious on the floor. She was suffering from malnutrition, having eaten little in two weeks. When her landlord was unable to arouse her, he called the police. Mrs. Bell refused to leave the house to go to the hospital, but she did accept some food and care from the neighbors. The landlord called the protective service agency. The caseworker learned that the woman had been the eldest of a large family. When she was very young, she had been placed with a white family to work as a servant. They took her with them when they moved to the city and she later became the personal servant of one of the daughters. She lost contact with her own family as she was illiterate and unable to afford trips home. She worked in domestic service all of her life and established few relationships outside of the employer's family. Even her brief marriage had been to another servant who also lived with the family.

Mrs. Bell's last employer, who had been dead for five years when she was referred to the protective service agency, had left her a legacy of $2,000. At the age of seventy-seven, she was thrown out into a world that she did not understand and she was cut off from the people she knew. For a brief period, she had worked as a maid and established minimum Social Security benefits of $33.50. As she did not understand that she could receive Old Age Assistance and Social Security at the same time, she was trying to live on the Social Security and her savings so that they would last for the rest of her life. She would pay rent and utilities from the check and withdraw about $30 a month from the savings for food and other items. When she was found, she had about $150 left from her inheritance, but she had grown too weak to go to the bank to make a withdrawal. She had been incontinent, and the floor was soiled. She kept a large stick in her bed so she could fight off the rats at night.

She trusted the protective service caseworker more than her neighbors or landlord. The caseworker was permitted to go through Mrs. Bell's papers and there found an old letter from a younger brother. When he was traced through the address on the letter, it was found that he had become quite a prominent businessman, and he responded immediately to the caseworker's call. As he had not heard from his sister in fifteen years, he had thought she was dead. As they were the only survivors of their family, he came immediately to help the caseworker move his sister to a custodial home for aged. He disposed of her personal belongings, paid for her medical care and even made arrangements for payment of her funeral expenses.

The caseworker made a referral to Old Age Assistance and provided the public welfare agency with the information they needed to establish eligibility.

Even with the brother's help, Mrs. Bell was reluctant to go to a home. However, the caseworker had learned that Mrs. Bell was more concerned that her hair had not been "pressed" in months than she was about her malnourished condition. She said she had never appeared before others without her hair straightened and pulled back with combs and without a starched white apron. Arrangements were made for these two requirements to be met as soon as she got to the home. With this assurance that her personal needs would be recognized, she accepted the plan willingly. In a short time, her health improved immeasurably and she joined a choir with the other residents. Her brother began to write her regularly and to make personal visits.

Initial Classifications: Functional: incompetent. Environmental: dangerous.

Final Classifications: Functional: marginally incompetent. Environmental: safe and protected.

Case III.   Mr. Clarke: Exploitation Prevented Through Guardianship and Protective Care

Mr. Clarke, a sixty-eight-year-old black male, was referred to the protective service agency by a nursing home administrator. He had had a serious stroke and had been treated at a general hospital, from which he was transferred to the nursing home. He could give no information about himself except his name, and the name of the barber who had cut his hair. The barbershop was located on a main street of the ghetto section.

After considerable investigation, the social worker located the barber and learned that Mr. Clarke had a host of friends who had not known what had happened to him. He had been working before he became ill. When the social worker located his papers and his age was verified, he was certified for Old Age Assistance. She then learned that he was eligible for a lump-sum Social Security payment. When this fact became known, "old friends" began to come forward claiming that he owed them money and offering to take care of him. He was released from the nursing home and wandered from house and house, living with different people and promising all of them money when he got his check. It was obvious to the social worker that he was incapable of handling his money and that he would be exploited.

She took him to a psychiatrist, who declared him incompetent. After it was explained to Mr. Clarke what this meant, he accepted the need for a guardian, and he helped the social worker locate an old friend who he felt could be trusted, an elderly woman who kept roomers. She agreed to care for him and her daughter, a schoolteacher, was willing to serve as guardian.

Part of the back Social Security payment was used to purchase the funeral of his choice, and the remainder was placed in a special account for emergencies. The social worker supported the guardian as she defended Mr. Clarke against the "friends" who had tried to exploit him. Mr. Clarke was delighted that there was enough money to purchase an entire new wardrobe, so he could go to church regularly. He had both care and freedom in his foster home.

Initial Classifications: Functional: incompetent. Environmental: potentially unsafe.

Final Classifications: Functional: incompetent. Environmental: protected.

Case IV. Mrs. Dodd: Protection Through Psychiatric Treatment and Family Care

Mrs. Dodd, a white female aged sixty-eight, was referred to the protective service agency by her brother, seventy-one. Her husband had died suddenly six weeks earlier, but the brother who lived in another town had not been notified. When he learned of the death, he and his wife came immediately. Friends reported that Mrs. Dodd had acted strangely for several years before her husband's death. She was so disturbed during the funeral that she laughed all through the service and tried to climb into the coffin. Nothing had been done to settle Mr. Dodd's estate, but since his death, Mrs. Dodd had purchased a color television set, a new bedroom suite and an expensive lawnmower-tractor. She was agitated, elated and irrational. At one time, she threatened the social worker with a sickle. Her husband's valuable tools and his boat and motor had been stolen or given away.

The social worker went with the brother to file an application for a mental health examination. They accompanied the deputies when they went to pick her up. She had to be restrained. She was transferred from the county psychiatric ward to a research psychiatric institute. A complete examination indicated that she had an inoperable abnormality of the brain. However, her behavior stabilized with medication. The brother accepted guardianship and began to secure her estate. After two months in the hospital, she was placed in an excellent custodial home for the aged where she could have her own furniture, and was allowed considerable freedom. There she improved so much that she could participate in planning for her future. She asked to be moved to a foster home, as it was cheaper and there would be more individualized service.

There had been a strained relationship between Mrs. Dodd and her brother for years, but his wife was very fond of her. The social worker was gradually able to help him understand his sister better and his attitude became more sympathetic. Several months later, the brother and sister-in-law decided to move to the city and take Mrs. Dodd into their own home so they could give her more personal supervision. The social worker assisted them in carrying through these plans.

Initial Classifications: Functional: dangerously incompetent. Environmental: unsafe.

Final Classifications: Functional: marginally incompetent. Environmental: protected.

Case V. Mr. Easton: Grief and Illness Require Protective Intervention

Mr. Easton, a white male aged eighty-one, had been a successful photographer. After his wife became ill and had to be placed in a nursing home, he deteriorated rapidly. He began to drink heavily and refused to pay the nursing home. When his wife died, he was too intoxicated to attend the funeral.

At the time of his referral for protective service, he drank constantly. On one occasion, he had set the house on fire. When he resisted all efforts to persuade him to accept a safer living plan, the landlord filed an eviction notice. The protective service worker went with the deputies who escorted him to a clinic for psychiatric observation. He was hostile and threatening. When his granddaughter was reached in another city, she completely supported the authoritative approach. After two days in the clinic, he was transferred to a hospital where it was found that he had a rare and severe kidney disease. He had surgery and a wide range of medical services.

His mental condition improved. The psychologist found that he had an IQ of 170 and had been a very creative person. He was placed in a nursing home where his medical program could be supervised and from which he could be taken to his clinic appointments. This home was in a remote area away from bars and liquor stores. After a short time, he made an excellent adjustment. When it was learned that he wished to write, a typewriter was obtained for him. He began writing stories for magazines and when the case was closed, he had completed four chapters of a book.

Initial Classification: Functional: dangerously incompetent. Environmental: potentially unsafe.

Final Classification: Functional: competent and self-determining.
Environmental: protected.

Case VI.   Mr. Frank: Exploitation of Illness and Incompetency

Mr. Frank, a white male aged sixty-eight, was referred to the agency by his divorced wife at the suggestion of the OAA caseworker. She and Mr. Frank had been legally divorced for fifteen years and separated for over twenty-one years, but Mrs. Frank had continued to be involved in his life. She had rescued him numerous times when he was "broke" and sick, and she still considered that he was her husband. Mr. Frank had been an excellent machinist and a thirty-second degree Mason before he succumbed to alcoholism. On one occasion, he had thrown their nine-year-old son down the stairs during a drunken rage. This episode resulted in their separation. Years later, when he developed tuberculosis, she arranged for him to enter a hospital, visited him and supplied his personal needs. The son, now thirty, characterized by his mother as a "nervous wreck," had never married, blamed his father for his problems and refused to have any contact with him.

Mrs. Frank had received a call from a neighbor that her husband was very ill. The relative she sent to see about him reported that Mr. Frank was living in squalor and being cared for by an alcoholic "nurse." The relative reported that he had apparently been drinking and had been unable to eat for two weeks. Mrs. Frank feared that his tuberculosis was reactivated. She was willing to take any action to get him under care, including filing a mental health petition with the court.

The doctor at the tuberculosis clinic reported that Mr. Frank's initial condition had been far advanced and more than likely was reactivated. There was no bed available at the tuberculosis hospital and with this suspicion of tuberculosis, he could not be admitted to a private hospital. The only alternative was to take him to the emergency room of the charity hospital where he could be placed in isolation. The caseworker requested that the public health nurse meet her at the house to give her opinion.

Mr. Frank was living in an upstairs garage apartment with window-panes missing and the stairs so broken that it was dangerous to climb them. The "nurse" was hostile, appeared to be suffering from a "hangover" and was frightened. Mr. Frank was confused and very sick. The public health nurse's examination indicated that his tuberculosis was probably reactivated and that he might be seriously ill. The caseworker returned to the office to get her supervisor. They both wore masks, and this had a dramatic effect on the "nurse," the client, various persons who wandered in and out, and later on the staff at the hospital.

At the second visit, the "nurse" appeared more frightened and less hostile. She said she had been hired by the Old Age Assistance caseworker to care for Mr. Frank and was supposed to be paid $50 a month. She seemed to be afraid that Mr. Frank was dying and that she would be held responsible. An ambulance was called, and Mr. Frank was much too sick to make more than a feeble protest. During the long wait, the "nurse" lost some of her fear and began to wonder what was to happen to her. She claimed that Mr. Frank had not paid her for three months and that she had bought most of the food out of her own money. A Social Security check of $73 was due the following day, and she was told that she could bring it to the hospital and have him sign it to apply on his legitimate bills.

Mr. Frank was taken to the hospital and put in seclusion. The doctor was given a history and told not to release him without calling the protective service worker. Since it was Friday afternoon, the social worker had her home and office number put on the chart. The doctor called at six o'clock the following morning and said that Mr. Frank did not have tuberculosis and was ready for discharge. The social worker persuaded a private hospital and doctor to accept him and met him there to admit him (his Medicare and Medicaid numbers had been obtained from the OAA record). The emergency room staff at the hospital had allowed him to fall out of bed and he had cut his head, an injury which required eight stitches. He was completely dehydrated, had a blocked kidney, was delirious and running a high fever. He was on the critical list for a week. His ex-wife and son went to the hospital the following day. The son reluctantly talked to the social worker and was given some help with his feelings. He agreed, as the next of kin, to support the protective service agency in any action that was necessary.

The Old Age Assistance checks were held pending future planning. As soon as Mr. Frank was conscious, he signed a change of address (with witnesses) for his Social Security check, but since it was likely that it would not be effective on the next check, he also signed (with witnesses) a post office change of address card. These were sent, with a letter, to the superintendent of the branch post office. When the post office refused to let her have the check, the "nurse" claimed to the post office clerk, the hospital, the social worker and Mr. Frank's ex-wife that she was his common-law wife and threatened to remove him from the hospital.

The protective service worker reminded her that she had said in front of witnesses that she was a hired nurse and that she was listed on the Old Age Assistance records as a hired nurse.

A private attorney for the "nurse" called the social worker and was quite hostile because the agency was not willing to recognize state laws on common-law marriages and her rights under these laws. The situation was explained to him and he finally agreed that she had not been very smart about thinking ahead if she intended to make such a claim.

A postal inspector also called, wanting to know what right the agency had to cash and use this man's checks and who had signed the change of address. The situation was explained, including the letter of incompetency and the pending change of payee. He made a personal visit to the branch post office to make sure that the "nurse" would not be given any further mail for Mr. Frank.

Mr. Frank did not regain ability to function mentally. A complete neurological examination revealed severe brain damage, diffused and irreversible. The doctor wrote a letter declaring him incompetent. A copy was sent to the Social Security board, requesting appointment of a change of payee.

Guardianship was considered but was deemed unnecessary at the time.

The Social Security board accepted Mrs. Frank as representative payee. Mr. Frank improved physically and was placed in a nursing home close to his former wife and son. The son was so impressed that his father was considered worthy of such aggressive protective action that he began to accept his father with more compassion. He began to visit him voluntarily and has sought out the doctor for a conference.

Initial Classifications: Functional: dangerously incompetent. Environmental: dangerous.

Final Classifications: Functional: incompetent. Environmental: protected.

Case VII.   Miss George

Miss George was still beautiful at eighty-nine and when she was sober, she was cultured and artistic. There were no known relatives. She came from a wealthy French family, was educated in private schools and had been in show business when she was quite young. Miss George had a love affair with a wealthy manufacturer when she was young and he provided for her amply during his lifetime. When he died, she was seventy years old and was left without funds or means of support. Brief periods of employment had qualified her for the minimum Social Security and she was dependent on this and Old Age Assistance. She had no notion of the value of money and spent her first two checks the first week after they were received. She would manage the rest of the month by begging and by selling or pawning her jewels. The trustees of her benefactor's estate had known of their relationship and sent her money from time to time in answer to her pleas. Drinking had been a part of her life from childhood but as she grew older, she had a lower tolerance for alcohol. She could be found staggering down a busy street or dancing naked on the lawn.

Her pattern of living was to move into a rooming house, paying a week's rent. After she became entrenched, she would count upon the landlord's reluctance to evict an "old woman." She could often manage to stay as long as six months before she would be forced to move. On one occasion, her priest and the church members moved her to a nursing home and paid for a month's care. She stayed two days after talking the operator into loaning her enough money to call a cab. Her friends still tried to help her but she exploited them to such an extent that they were forced to discontinue this help.

Miss George was referred to the protective service agency at the time of an eviction and was moved to a boarding house that specialized in aged people. Each month, there was a hassle with her to get her to pay her bill. Her drinking increased and she was often disabled because of it. It was learned that the trustees of her friend's estate had considerable latitude in how much money they allowed her. They agreed to send the agency a certain sum of money each month to be administered for her. She still needed guardianship over her other money. No one would assume this responsibility because it was known that she would make life miserable for anyone who had control over her money. Finally, she was arrested for shoplifting. This arrest made the need for guardianship more apparent and one old friend reluctantly accepted the responsibility. The agency then managed all of her money by agreement with the guardian. The caseworker refused to allow her to have cash that could be used for alcohol but was quite indulgent in meeting her needs and providing special treats and comforts. She accepted this turn of events with all of the zest of a child playing a new game and enjoyed testing the caseworker and finding ways around the limitations. By controlling the money, the drinking was curtailed. With an improved diet and living arrangements, her general well-being improved. She now lives a fantasy of a "woman of means" whose "trustee" sees to her needs and does not bother her with demeaning details.

Initial Classifications: Functional: incompetent. Environmental: dangerous.

Final Classifications: Functional: incompetent. Environmental: manageable.

Case VIII. Mrs. Hill: The Difficulties of Securing Correct Diagnosis and Appropriate Treatment

Neighbors called the protective service agency when they had not seen Mr. and Mrs. Hill, both in their eighties, for several days and no one had answered the telephone or the doorbell.

Convincing the police that this was an emergency, the protective service worker had the door unlocked. Mrs. Hill was found on the floor unconscious. Her husband was dead in bed.

Mrs. Hill was sent to the emergency ward of the nearest hospital. When she was revived, she became greatly agitated as she insisted that she must go home to her ill husband. The examining doctor at the private hospital ordered the medical social worker to have the patient moved to the general hospital's psychiatric ward. He said her condition was due to "senility" and denied that there was a medical problem.

The protective service worker was informed of the doctor's orders, but he was unable to secure a bed at the general hospital immediately. Finally, two days later, it was possible to move Mrs. Hill to the general hospital. There the admitting doctor found the patient in an advanced stage of malnutrition and dehydration. (She had been given no liquids or food during the stay at the previous hospital.) It was obvious to the examining physician that the patient had been under sedation while she was at the first hospital.

As Mrs. Hill was in critical condition and the body of her husband was awaiting burial, the protective service worker attempted to find relatives or friends. He finally located one friend; no relatives could be found. The landlord, who was concerned about one month's rent, was attempting to become administrator of the estate. As the house was being closed by the friend and the protective service worker, $3,000 in uncashed Social Security checks, some stocks, and $14,000 in a savings account were discovered. Arrangements were made for Mr. Hill's funeral which was attended by the friend and the protective service worker.

In the meantime, Mrs. Hill, who was declared "impaired in intellect and judgment" by a psychiatric diagnosis, was sent by the general hospital to a city custodial facility. When the protective service agency learned about this, arrangements were made to move Mrs. Hill to a nursing home. She was improving, but she continued to need nursing care. At the time of the report, the protective service agency had been unable to locate relatives or other friends. Plans were being made for guardianship.

Initial Classifications: Functional: incompetent. Environmental: dangerous.

Final Classifications: Functional: incompetent. Environmental: protected.

Members of NCOA Protective Service Project Advisory Committee

Chairman: Hugh A. Ross
Professor of Law
Thomas Franklin Backus School of Law
Case Western Reserve University
Cleveland, Ohio

Miss Martha Adam
Mrs. Betty H. Anderson
Delwin Anderson
Louis L. Bennett
James J. Burr
Mrs. Herbert E. Dobbs
Mrs. Roy W. Engle
Albert S. Epstein
William C. Fitch
William E. Friedman
Mrs. Joe Bales Graber, M.P.H.
Miss Mary L. Hemmy
Dr. John G. Hill
Lowell Iberg
Claude L. Kordus
Abraham Kostick
Irving J. Ladimer, S.J.D.
*Miss Neota Larson

Leroy P. Levitt, M.D.
Mrs. Elizabeth Mac Latchie
Dr. Robert Morris
Mrs. Virginia O'Neill
Mrs. Annie May Pemberton, ACSW
Leon L. Rackow, M.D.
Miss Ollie A. Randall
Mrs. Eva M. Reese
Miss Rosemary Reynolds
Simon Rosenzweig
*Mrs. Ruth B. Taylor
Prescott W. Thompson, M.D.
Mrs. Helen Turner
Herbert J. Weiss, M.D.
Mrs. Ruth A. White
Ernest F. Witte, Ph.D.
Miss Elizabeth Wood

_____

* Now deceased.

INDEX